RESTORATION and PHOTOGRAPHIC COPYING

To my father, Edward M. Shafran, a pioneer in the field of Photo-Restoration.

PREFACE

The copying and restoring of photographs that are damaged, faded, or that have deteriorated with the passage of time, is a photographic specialty requiring the skills of the photographer and the photo-retoucher-artist. It is a little-known craft, even among professional photographers, because of the scarcity of professional photo-restoration specialists and the absence of publicity about the subject. Also, only a small percentage of the millions upon millions of photographs that have been made in the past hundred years or so, both by professionals and amateurs, are considered valuable enough for copy-restoration.

Which photographs merit consideration for such copy-restoration? Note the use of the term "copy-restoration." It is not practical, except in a very few instances, to do the restoration work upon, or to, the original old photograph. This is usually copied photographically and the re-touching or restoring is done upon a copy print. There are those photographs that have a historical value and are kept in archives, museums, libraries, etc., for the visual insight they can shed upon a certain historical period. Then there are those that are personal property and are of sentimental value only to their owners. A daguerreotype of Abraham Lincoln will interest scholars, historians, the general public, etc., while one of an unknown Washington, D. C. shopkeeper, taken about the same time, will only be of genuine interest to his descendants. A snapshot taken during World War II that shows General Eisenhower could have some historical value and be of general interest, whereas the many snapshots taken of the private soldiers can only be of personal importance to these men or their families.

Since the pictures kept in archives and museums are treated as valuable items and are properly cared for, there is seldom any need to restore them. However, many of the photos in the possession of private individuals are kept carelessly, in basements or attics, loosely or cast about, so that they are subject to the deteriorating influences of dampness and humidity, to breaking, tearing, folding, etc., and the destructive tendencies of children. Therefore, the majority of those original photographs presented for copy-restoration are these privately owned ones.

The art or craft of photo-restoration is one that has evolved through the years. Its beginnings can be traced back to a period around the end of the 19th and beginning of the 20th century. At that time, a big business was being done making enlarged portraits from the daguerreotypes, tintypes, photo studio prints, and the newly emerging snapshots that were in the possession of the public. The customer's originals were sent to special enlarging houses in several big cities, where they were copied and "blown up." Since these enlargements were made on the flat or faded side, with some photographic quality and detail lost because of limitations of the copy film and enlarging paper then available, they had to be strengthened and worked up by hand with pastels or charcoal. Many were tinted or colored by pastel. Then the air brush came upon the scene and this instrument began to be used to finish these enlargements through the use of dilutions of water color. Then most of the original photographs were relatively new and in good condition, so that all that was necessary was to strengthen or color the enlarged copies. However, in time, some originals came through with cracks or spots and the artist found himself having to eliminate or correct these by retouching. The orders for the copy enlargements were taken on by door-to-door salesmen who would send them on to the copy house. In their eagerness to get the order, they would promise almost anything the customer wanted. They accepted orders to change clothing, to make regroupings, to remove a person from a group for a portrait of that person by himself, to take off hats, etc. The artists, having to make good on the salesmen's promises, developed the techniques for making those alterations.

Today the techniques for photo-restoration have undergone little change. The copying procedure is the same now at it was then, although better equipment and a greater variety of films are available, so the photo-restorer can accomplish more to improve the copy in this step than he could have fifty years ago. The print upon which the retoucher-artist works is still a photo enlargement. Here too a greater variety of paper grades and surfaces are available. More advanced printing techniques have been developed, so much more improvement and correction work can now be accomplished while printing than could have been done years ago. The air brush is still the basic retouching and restoring tool and is used in much the same way it was originally. However, because of the passage of time, many original photographs have deteriorated and become damaged, thus requiring a greater amount of restoration, demanding more skill and patience on the part of the photo-restorer, and presenting him with more difficult problems than his predecessor came across.

In the past, this craft was learned via the age-old road of apprenticeship. Today this is not the case. And there are no special courses available in colleges, art schools, or photographic institutes. This book, to my knowledge, is the first one that has ever been written exclusively on the subject. There have been other works on retouching or airbrushing that may have touched briefly on the subject but have not gone into it with the detail it requires. This is a basic text, therefore, on the art or craft of copy photo-restoration.

This will interest photographers in all branches of the profession. Those who do general studio work with an emphasis on portraiture are the most likely to be involved with photo-restorations. Their clientele possesses such damaged photographs of sentimental value. When someone outside the photographic field has such a picture, to whom can he turn for its restoration? Obviously, the photographer. Photographers working in the commercial, industrial, news, and other special branches will also find an occasion when the problem of photo-restoration arises.

There is also no reason why the serious and advanced nonprofessional or hobbyist should not interest himself in this subject and attempt to copy and restore photographs.

The process requires the skills and talents inherent to photography, to retouching, and to drawing. The first is to take care of copying the original photograph and making the new print for retouching purposes. The second is to work out the damages and blemishes by the use of retouching pencils, etching knives, airbrush, and/or any other applicable tool. The third is to work in the outline and masses of any picture area that might be missing or blotted out and needs to be replaced.

There are many service specialists in the field of photography, such as retouchers, colorists, and airbrush artists. They provide these services professionally to the general-purpose studio or commercial photographer, who cannot do or does not have the time for, this work. To such specialists the study and practice of photo-restoration should be a relatively simple matter, inasmuch as they are already acquainted with the basic required skills.

At the time of this writing there are only a handful of specialists working in this field. There are several reasons for this. One is that many of the "old timers" have retired, without having trained assistants to replace them. In former times there were many students who would have been glad to undergo a period of apprenticeship at a nominal salary, or none at all at first, in order to learn a trade. Today this is not so. Photographic schools and art academies have either not considered the subject important or popular enough to merit a course of instruction, or have been unable to find qualified personnel to teach it. Also, this specialty has been "hiding its light under a bushel." There has been no recruiting on the part of those in the trade and no aspirants, since there is little awareness of the existence of photo-restoration as a craft, or of the commercial possibilities of it.

So the appearance of a book, such as this, devoted solely to the subject of copy photo-restoration is overdue. Restoration and photographic copying is designed to present the subject to you from a practical viewpoint derived from over three decades of experience, practical experience actually producing photo-restorations. It does not wander into any theoretical dissertations, for the sake of being wordy, but rather tries to come to the point. That point being that following the guidelines it offers, providing one has the necessary talents and abilities, the reader should be able to set out on the road to doing copy photo-restoration work. While the steps involving copying the original and making the enlarged workprint are discussed in special chapters, such discussion deals only with those subjects as they relate to photo-restoration. There is no complete examination of all aspects of photographic copying or of enlarging. Other books, discussing these subjects in detail, exist. It is more fitting to devote these pages to the subject in question rather than going farther afield.

Reading and studying this book will not, of itself, make a photo-restorer of you. No book can be expected to do that. The how-to-do-it book on taking pictures will not make a photographer of the reader who knows little or nothing of that subject. But it should afford him a good idea of what photography is, tell him what he should do, and how he should go about it, thus putting him on the road to making good photos. Reading is but the beginning. Doing and practicing must follow. Going ahead without a book of instructions is like driving in a strange country without a roadmap.

This book should not only be such a "roadmap" to the photographer, retoucher, photo-colorist and photographer's artist, but also to studio receptionists, camera store owners, and sales personnel, photo finishers, operators of picture framing and art shops, to anyone in the business of servicing the public with pictures and photographs, to anyone who is likely to encounter the request or necessity for restoring a damaged photograph.

It also should be helpful to those institutions that maintain archives and possess files of valuable and historical photographs, some of which may be fading or deteriorating, by showing how these can be restored or preserved.

CONTENTS

1 WHAT WE MEAN BY PHOTO-RESTORATION 13

2 PRE-COPY TREATMENT OF ORIGINAL PHOTOGRAPHS . . 24

3 COPYING 58

4 RETOUCHING AND ARTWORK ON THE COPY NEGATIVE 77

5 MAKING THE WORKPRINT . . . 91

6 POSITIVE RETOUCHING AND RESTORATION WORK ON THE WORKPRINT 106

7 RECOPYING 153

8 THE AIRBRUSH 163

9 CONCLUSION 177

1. A typical sampling of old photographs that are presented to the photographer for copying and restoration.

CHAPTER 1

WHAT WE MEAN BY PHOTO-RESTORATION

The term "photo-restoration" is a misnomer. Actually, photo-restoration does not involve restoring the damaged or faded photograph to its original or new condition. Rather, it involves making a copy of that photograph and creating, or re-creating, a new picture while removing blemishes and faults by photographic means or by artwork and retouching.

The deterioration that affects a photograph can be of a physical nature, a chemical one, or both. It can happen to a photograph that was made many years ago, such as a daguerreotype, or quite recently, such as a color snapshot.

Physical deterioration includes cracks, tears, breaks, pencil or ink marks, scratches, abrasions, etc. These usually result from careless handling and improper storage. Chemical deterioration includes discoloration, fading, silver oxidation or exudation, water, fire, smoke, or dirt stains. These effects are due to exposure, dampness or moisture, the passage of time, improper processing, oxidation, or fire or flood.

These faults should be corrected by photographic means whenever possible. Whatever cannot be corrected photographically must be remedied by retouching and artwork. The use of color filters, when copying the original photograph, can reduce and sometimes eliminate the effect of discoloraton and stains. Special contrast films and filters can bring out and strengthen faded details. Cleaning the print before copying and using polarized lights can reduce the effect of exudation.

Physical damage, such as cracks, breaks, and tears, cannot be eliminated by photography alone, since these faults will show up on the copy photograph. However, since this is a new print with an undamaged surface, unlike the original, the cracks and tears can be removed, or covered, by retouching with pencil, spotting brush, and air brush.

There are seven basic steps in the process of making a restored photograph. These are (1) pre-copy work; (2) making the copy negative; (3) retouching the copy negative; (4) making a workprint; (5) finishing or retouching the workprint; (6) recopying the workprint; (7) making the final print.

Pre-copy work involves treating or cleaning the original photograph prior to copying. Often old photographs are coated with a layer of soot, dirt, or grime that can be removed, sometimes completely, by proper cleaning. After cleaning, if the surface of the original is otherwise unmarred, a good copy negative can be obtained that can produce a print that requires no further work. But this is not often the case. If the original has been allowed to become so dirt-ridden and begrimed, it is probable that it has also fallen prey to cracks, scratches, and breaks, which

2. A daguerreotype, circa 1860, in need of restoration.

3. A restored copy inserted in the original case to supplant the damaged original.

4. A restored copy finished to a rectangular shape with a new background added.

5. Restored copy finished as a full bust portrait.

6. Restored copy finished as a vignetted bust portrait.

copying alone will not eliminate and which will require retouching and artwork.

In order to make the copy negative, a photographic arrangement consisting of a view camera, copy lights, and a copyboard is required. Its purpose is to photograph the original picture so that a reproduction print, or copy print, can be made. While copying, some corrective work can be accomplished. Sometimes this can be enough to produce a print that requires little or no additional work.

Before making the reproduction print (which may be used as a workprint or as a final print, depending upon the amount of required restoration work), the copy negative should be examined to see if any retouching, airbrushing, or artwork can be done upon it to help make a better print. In the case of cracks that are not too prominent, or small spots, such work will be enough to produce a print that requires no more retouching or artwork. Even if this is not the case, the work accomplished on the copy negative can save the photo-restorer later work, when the workprint is being retouched.

7. A damaged group photograph, circa 1880.

Making the workprint involves more effort than may be needed to make an ordinary enlarged print. Some planning is necessary. The proper use of cropping, dodging, vignetting, and masking can do much to reduce the amount of retouching and artwork that will be required to finish the workprint. The best size for the workprint has to be determined. It should be large enough to permit detail work to be accomplished; it should not be enlarged to a size that will cause too much diffusion. This is especially true when working from small originals. The type of photographic surface needed to produce the optimum artwork results must also be considered.

The most important step, the one that requires the most skill and involves the greatest amount of work, is that of finishing and restoring the workprint. Whenever much restoration work is necessary, where new artwork is required, as in the case of adding clothing or changing backgrounds, the best way to accomplish this is by positive retouching on the workprint. This is done with the aid of hand retouching tools, such as pencils, etching knives, spotting brushes, etc. The most valuable tool

8. A restored copy of this group. Note the addition of foreground and roof area by artwork to provide a squarer format.

is the air brush, without which most restoration jobs will prove so difficult and time consuming that they would be impractical.

Because of the odd appearance (due to the off colors of the air brush whites and grays) of the air brush-finished workprint, which differs from that of an ordinary print, and because of the possibility of rubbing off this artwork or spoiling it by handling, it is necessary to recopy. The resultant negative is called the recopy or the restored negative. It can be used to produce any number of final or finished prints, in any size, upon any surface, and in any tone desired.

Making prints from recopy negatives requires a somewhat different treatment than printing from ordinary negatives. Because these are copy negatives, they will often be flatter than regular portrait negatives and they may tend not to be as snappy or lively. So care as to the choice of papers, tones, etc., is essential. Some additional spotting or touching up may be necessary, as something may have been overlooked or neglected in the finishing of the workprint.

Certain tools are required by the photo-restorer. Of course, the ability to use these tools is essential. Without them, the photo-restorer's skill can accomplish nothing. With the proper tools, the skill can be acquired. These tools can be divided into two categories: photographic tools and art tools.

In the category of photographic tools, equipment to make copy negatives is needed. The most important is the copy camera. This can be a basic view camera with provision for extending the bellows. For best results you should have a permanent copy set-up, with such accessories as a track for guiding the camera, a copyboard for holding the material to be photographed, and copy lights to illuminate the material. Then you need film holders and color filters. Of course, a complete darkroom is essential for processing the films.

Next, we should consider the equipment necessary for making prints. Included are the enlarger (the basic item) and all the equipment for developing and processing prints. In the discussion on making these workprints, we will only touch the subject as it relates to making photographic prints for restoration purposes. It is assumed that you know how to make prints and enlargements. If you do not, there is much literature on this subject that does a better job than we can and that makes going into the subject superfluous to the discussion of photo-restoration.

A variety of tools is needed to accomplish the retouching and artwork that has to be done on the workprint. The basic and most important of these is the air brush. The type of air brush used by the photo-restorer

9. A restored copy of the little girl sitting in the doorway, removing her from the group by copying and cropping the workprint, providing a small bench and new background by artwork.

10. A restored copy of the father, removing him from the group by copying and cropping the workprint, removing the child from his arm, replacing the covered portion of his beard, and adding new clothing by artwork.

11. A regroup portrait of the father and mother, placing them closer together by adjustment of the copy negative; removing children and adding clothing by artwork.

12. An old photograph in good condition. This requires no artwork.

is a fine instrument about the size of a fountain pen that can apply color or paint to the surface of a print in the form of a fine line, a dot or series of dots, a broad tint or wash, or as a heavy covering color or tone.

The air brush cannot work unless it is backed up by a source of air pressure. This can be either an air compressor or a tank of compressed air. An easel or drawing board is needed to hold the picture being worked on. Pencils, spotting brushes, erasers, pastels, tortillons, opaque and transparent water colors, etching knives, and friskets are some of the additional art aids that you must have. These will be discussed later in more detail.

13. An old photograph in poor condition, which will require artwork and retouching.

These tools are important. So is the skill necessary to use them properly. What skills must the photo-restorer have? He must wear three hats—that of the photographer, that of the retoucher, and that of the artist—because his craft requires the knowledge of photography, retouching, and artwork.

As a photographer, he must be able to make good copy negatives from any photograph. He must know what films and filters to use. He must know how to make enlarged prints from his copy negatives and how to dodge, vignette, and crop these prints. He must know how to do his processing work in the darkroom.

Retouching is used by photographers to overcome and correct faults and blemishes in a picture. Portrait photographers make use of negative retouching to remove blemishes from a subject's face, to soften wrinkles and age lines, and to remove accidental spots and pinholes in the negative. This type of work can be done on the print and is known as positive retouching.

The simplest type of retouching is spotting. This is done by putting the lead or paint, with a finely pointed pencil or a very fine spotting brush, into the white area that creates the spot. Anyone can do this, if he is careful, patient, and takes his time. Softening wrinkles and hard lines requires more skill and the ability to use the retouching tools to blend the light and dark areas to obtain a smooth and pleasing effect. The photo-restorer must be able to do this.

The air brush is, in essence, a retouching tool. Its capabilities allow the retoucher much more latitude than does the pencil, etching knife, or spotting brush. It is a difficult tool to master, but without it the photo-restorer would find it impractical, if not impossible, to complete most restoration jobs. So, in addition to being a photographer and retoucher, the photo-restorer must be a proficient air-brush operator or air-brush artist.

There will be some cases in which photography and retouching are not enough to complete a job. Real artwork is usually required where part of the original picture is missing. The only way to replace this missing part is by drawing it in and rendering it in such a manner that it becomes part of the new picture and does not seem to be a patch. It may also be necessary to extend the edges of a picture where an original has been trimmed too close to the main subject and the effect is a crowded one. There are also instances where the photo-restorer is required to change a subject's clothing by adding a suit or a dress. He may be called upon to add a new background, replace a missing arm, leg, or ear, or open a closed eye. This requires artistic ability and it is essential, therefore, that the photo-restorer has some art training and background.

Now it should be added that photo-restoration need not be the result of only one person's work; it can be a team effort. One party can do the photographic work and the other can do the artwork. In a large commercial photographic organization, which may handle many restoration jobs, the work can be divided into tasks and a production line set up. Or a skilled air-brush artist who finds his time occupied at the easel might have someone else do the copying and printing for him. The photographer who does not have the time or skill to do the retouching and artwork can have someone qualified do this for him.

But no matter who does the job, or how many persons are involved, the basic requirements remain the same—skill in photography, skill in retouching, and skill in artwork.

In the chapters that follow, we shall discuss in more detail the steps and stages of the photo-restoration process from pre-copy treatment through copying, work on the copy negative, workprints, restoration finishing, recopying, and making final prints.

CHAPTER 2

PRE-COPY TREATMENT OF ORIGINAL PHOTOGRAPHS

It was stated earlier that in photo-restoration the original photograph itself is not rejuvenated, but a photographic reproduction is retouched and restored. However, this should not imply that nothing can or should be done to that original to improve its condition and help the photo-restorer obtain a better copy. While we cannot hope to be able to restore it completely, we may be able to improve it partially. We say, "may be able to improve it," because there are originals in such bad condition, so fragile and worn, that they cannot be treated or improved. We dare not do so lest they virtually disintegrate.

In each step of the photo-restoration process, we want to take particular pains to get the best results possible at that stage. The attitude of letting results slide because we can hope to rectify the lapse in a later step of the process is a bad one. That is why pre-copy cleaning is important. The original that has not been cleaned or prepared as well as it could have been will not produce the best or cleanest possible copy negative. And an inferior copy negative will produce an inferior print. What the workprint lacks has to be replaced by artwork. A blemish that has not been taken out by cleaning the original has to be removed by retouching. This means additional retouching and restoring work that could have been avoided.

Let us take a simple example. We have this old oval masked photo of a bearded gentleman. There is a large black smudge to the left of his

14. (LEFT) *An old photograph with a black mark, which consists of dirt or grease, covering part of the face.*

15. (RIGHT) *The same picture with the mark removed by cleaning.*

eye and above his cheek. There are also two similar smudges on his suit and sleeve. They can be dirt, grime, or grease. If they are, they can be removed by cleaning. If we do not remove this suspected dirt, it will show up in the copy, as it does in the illustration, and will have to be removed by retouching the negative, etching the print, air-brush opaquing, or a combination of these three methods. If we can clean the original, however, we will get the result illustrated and have a clean copy while avoiding much corrective work.

Of course, there are instances where such a mark cannot be removed by cleaning. In such cases the mark is not due to grease or removable dirt, but to some chemical or indelible substance. Then we have to try to eliminate it by using filters in copying or by retouching.

CHEMICAL DAMAGE

Checking for Dirt and Grime

All originals should be examined closely. What you are looking for, at this point, is dirt, soot, or grime that covers the surface of the picture and dims the image. Often this is not obvious and a detailed examination is required. The dirt forms a layer that lies on top of the emulsion. If it is a heavy or dark layer, it will be noticed. But, if it is a light layer, it may be overlooked. With experience, your eye will detect the presence of such a layer almost instinctively. Even so, you should test each original for dirt.

One simple test can be made by rubbing a portion of the print area with an Artgum, a kneaded, or any soft eraser. Even the eraser end of an ordinary pencil will do the job. It will pick up or rub off any dirt and will reveal a cleaner print underneath. In testing, the use of caution must be emphasized. You must be careful while using the eraser, for there is always a danger of removing part of the emulsion by rubbing with too much pressure. To minimize this, the testing should be done along the edges or outer areas of the original, not in the center or at any point that contains a vital detail.

A similar test can be made by using a diluted solution of ammonia or liquid soap. This is applied carefully to the original with a swab of cotton. A light rubbing or swabbing, using a circular motion, should pick up any dirt or grime, which should be readily visible on the cotton, and the cleaner print beneath the dirt should become apparent. Here, too, the test should be applied to the outer, or least important, areas of the picture.

It is very important, before testing or cleaning, to examine the surface of the original for any cracks, holes, or breaks in the emulsion. We must know whether or not this surface is marred. Why? Well, if we use the eraser for cleaning, no matter how gently we apply it, some pressure must be applied. This can aggravate any break or scar, causing the emulsion to lift up and spread the damage. This same danger exists when we use the cotton swab moistened with ammonia or liquid soap. Moistening softens the emulsion, especially around the break, so that when the cotton passes over the spot, it picks up and tears away the emulsion.

If the eraser does not produce a cleaner spot, or if the moist cotton does not pick up any dirt, you can conclude that there is no dirt layer and that there is no reason to attempt cleaning. But, if the test is positive, you should proceed to attempt cleaning, because a clean original will produce a better copy than a dirty one.

Cleaning by Eraser

Using the eraser is simple, since it merely involves rubbing the dirt off the surface of the picture. You should have a soft rubber eraser, an

Artgum, and a kneaded eraser, since it will usually be necessary to use all three. The rubber eraser, shaved to a point, can be used on smaller originals or to get into certain special local areas. The Artgum and kneaded erasers will be more helpful on wider areas or larger originals. No ink eraser or hard one of that type should ever be used, for these will scratch the picture.

A light touch is necessary. We mentioned the danger of using too much pressure. Even if the surface seems to be without any scratches or breaks, there is always the chance of damaging the emulsion and removing part of the image by rubbing too hard. You may find it necessary to go over the picture several times. Also, you may find that after cleaning the picture shows streaks that follow the strokes or direction of the eraser. This effect can be corrected by going over the entire picture with the kneaded rubber. Or, if this does not work, you can still go over the picture by swabbing with moist cotton.

Cleaning by Washing or Swabbing

When the original is of a larger size, the use of the eraser becomes impractical. Cotton that is moistened in a diluted solution of ammonia or of liquid soap is more efficient, since it covers the larger area more quickly.

The moistened cotton is applied to the print surface with a light touch. The print should be swabbed gently. If the dirt does not come off readily at first, you must not be tempted to resort to hard rubbing. This can pull off some of the emulsion. Rather, you should let the surface dry, then repeat the process with another piece of cotton moistened with the cleaning solution. Often the first attempt will serve to soften the dirt layer so that the second attempt cleans it off more easily. It is essential to allow the print to dry between the cleaning attempts so that the emulsion does not become too wet and soft.

We mentioned the instance where you have attempted to clean the original by the eraser method and are not satisfied with the results. This picture can be recleaned by washing. However, you must be more careful here. The rubbing could have created some scratches or ridges in the emulsion. You may not be able to see them, but they can be present and can allow the swabbing to pick up some of the emulsion. So, if you want to continue cleaning such a print by washing, you must do so with an extremely light touch.

A word of caution! Never try to soak these prints or immerse them in water with the hope that this will soften the dirt layer. It may only

16. The improvement that is obtained by cleaning a portion of a dirt-covered photograph.

cause the paper or cardboard backing to weaken or disintegrate. And never let too much water get on the surface of the original. The cotton should contain only enough of the solution to pick up the dirt; it should not leave a puddle on the print.

Cleaning Damaged Originals

Basically, cleaning the damaged original follows the procedure we have described above. However, aside from the fact that more care is necessary, the damaged original must be cleaned bit by bit in the local areas of the picture while the undamaged one can be cleaned as a whole or unit. In studying the damaged original, you should note those portions of the picture that are not damaged, where there are no cracks or holes. These parts should be cleaned first, one at a time. Your eraser or cotton swab should be fine enough to fit into such areas without touching the actual damage. If the print is cracked, work the undamaged portion almost up to the crack without touching it. If there is a hole, work around it, getting as close as possible without touching the edge.

We must emphasize that cotton or an eraser must not touch the damage. If they do, there is a strong possibility of the emulsion being picked up and torn away, thus increasing the size of the crack or damage. An important part of a picture can be lost this way, especially if the picture is of a group or contains much detail. When the original is cleaned in this manner, there will probably be a collar or rim of dirt along the edge of the damaged area. This cannot be helped. It will have to be corrected later by retouching either the copy negative or workprint. But this will involve less work than rebuilding any part of the picture that might have been torn away.

Stains

Stains that have formed on a picture are not dirt. They differ from dirt, grime, and grease and cannot be treated in the same way. As we have seen, dirt forms a coating on top of the actual picture surface, or emulsion, and can, in most cases, be removed by a rather simple cleaning procedure. A stain, on the other hand, has been absorbed into the very emulsion. It does not just lie on top of the surface, and thus cannot be removed by the same cleaning process.

Many stains are caused by a chemical change in the actual photograph, which is often due to the simple passage of time. Or it is due to improper or careless processing at the time the print was made. A print that has not been washed properly after fixing is bound to develop stains, turn brown, or fade within a relatively short period. The properly finished print may take decades to reach the same state. Thus we often find older photographs from past generations in much better shape, chemically speaking, than some prints that have been made in the past few years. Stains of this type cannot be removed by cleaning.

Theoretically, it could be possible to correct such a print by bleaching and redeveloping or by toning. For practical purposes, this is inadvisable and not recommended. It may only work if the print is in perfect physical condition. Then you have to determine if the printing paper is compatible with the chemicals you want to use. Instead of eliminating the stain, this treatment could emphasize it or have no effect on it at all. It should be remembered that these stains can be eliminated at a later time in copying or by retouching. This could take less time and involve less work than trying to treat the original print chemically by redeveloping or toning. The practical photo-restorer can use any one of several methods to correct certain faults. He will use the one that is the most efficient and that involves the least work, trouble, and risk. He usually only has one original photo to work from and he cannot afford to endanger it by experimentation.

Dampness and moisture also cause staining. This type of stain is usually brownish in tone. The dampness sets off chemical changes that cause the staining. It advances the effect of aging. If the print is mounted upon a cardboard, the cement or glue activated by the moisture will come through and stain the picture. These stains cannot be removed by cleaning, nor can bleaching, redeveloping, or toning be considered.

A number of other agents can and will stain the original print when they are brought into contact with it. These are ink, lipstick, food, paint, fire, and smoke. To remove them or reduce their effect, you must determine what they are and what caused them. Ink stains may be reduced by cleaning with water or alcohol. Lipstick may be removed by water and soap, or by carbon tetrachloride; the same is true for food stains. Turpentine or carbon tetrachloride can help if the paint had an oil base. Smoke stains can be removed, to some extent, by water and soap or by carbon tetrachloride. Such treatment should be applied locally, by touching the affected area with the cleaning agent. Do not get any on the unaffected area or it might create a new stain. Nothing can be done if fire has touched the print.

In treating these stains, you should be careful to use a light touch. If you try to remove a stain from clothing by using cleaning fluid, you have to rub hard to get out the stain. Do not do this with an old photograph. You will only rip off the emulsion.

The stained original is also very likely to have a layer of dirt. Cleaning, as described before, will remove the dirt, but not the stains. This might confuse you. When you clean such an original you must be able to sense when you have gotten rid of all the dirt possible and when to stop cleaning. If you continue the rubbing or washing in the attempt to get rid of the stain, you may only succeed in tearing off or wearing away some of the emulsion.

Treatment can reduce a stain; seldom will it remove the stain entirely. Never use any strange chemicals or bleaches. These can remove the entire picture and leave you with nothing to copy. But, if you can reduce the stain, it will be easier to eliminate the remaining part by filtering in making the copy or by retouching.

17. (ABOVE) *Portion of a photograph that is exuding grains of silver.*

18. (BELOW) *Improvement obtained by removing this grain by cleaning.*

Exudation

Another phenomenon that occurs to old photographs should be mentioned here. This is a peculiar one, to which the name "exudation" has been given. What occurs is that minute metallic specks form on the surface of the old photograph. This is due to the oxidation of the silver compounds in the emulsion that form the picture. These specks act as miniature reflecting surfaces that prevent our seeing the image clearly. Sometimes they are only visible when the picture is viewed from a side angle. However, these reflections are picked up by the copy lights and cause a glare effect that prevents our obtaining a good copy negative of the picture image. The negative records only the glare and not the picture that lies beneath the layer of metallic grain.

Fortunately, these granules are on the surface of the picture and can be removed without destroying or damaging the underlying image. They can be removed in much the same manner as that used for the removal of dirt and grime. That is, the layer of grain can be removed by rubbing it off with a kneaded or Artgum eraser, or it may be washed off with a cotton swab moistened with liquid soap or a mild solution of ammonia.

19. (LEFT) *The only available portions of a broken old crayon enlargement, pinned to copy board to show separate pieces.*

20. (RIGHT) *The same original with the separate portions joined by taping the back and attached to the copy board with pushpins.*

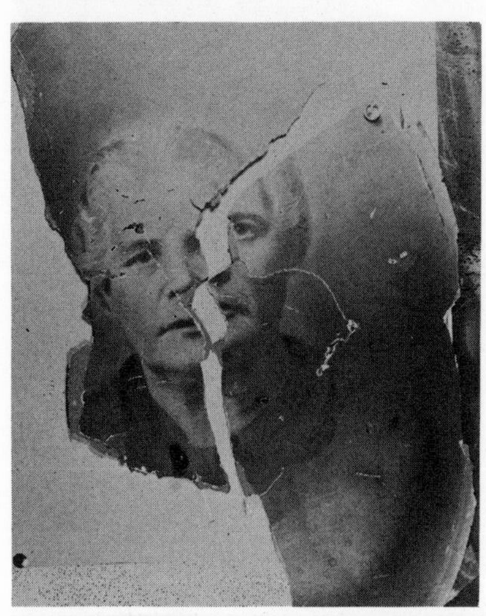

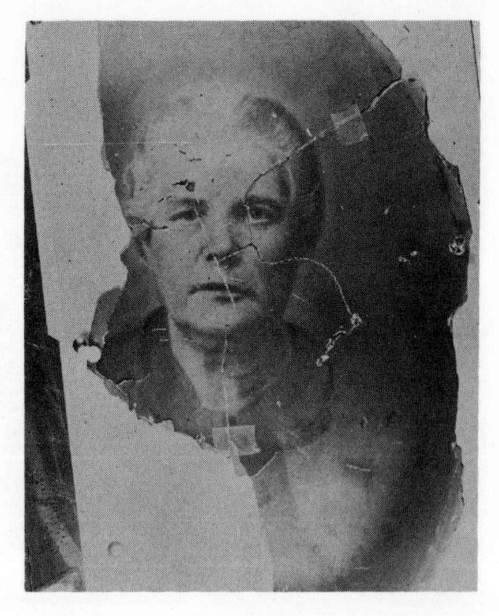

Unless the original is a small one, the use of the moistened cotton will prove much more practical than the use of erasers. Here, too, the same care and caution must be exercised as with the removal of dirt and grime. The original can be coated with a layer of dirt as well as that of the exuded silver grain. The same cleaning process will take care of both layers; it may only require a little more effort and time.

When the surface of the original, or that part of the original we want to copy, is in otherwise perfect condition—without cracks, damage, or dirt—the exudation effect can also be reduced or removed by the application of a thin coating of petroleum jelly. It acts to add a gloss to the print surface on which the reflecting grains are lost. The petroleum jelly should be rubbed on sparingly. If too much is used it will streak, and these streaks will be reflected as white lines on the copy negative. This method is practical only when the original is a small one and where there is absolutely no dirt present.

21. (LEFT) *A photograph which has been broken into three pieces.*

22. (CENTER) *The same picture pieced together by taping the back.*

23. (RIGHT) *The purpose of this illustration is to show why celluloid tape should never be placed on the surface of a broken original photograph.*

PHYSICAL DAMAGE

If we think of dirt, stains, and exudation as chemical deterioration of an original, then breaks, cracks, holes, etc., can be considered to be physical deterioration or damage. While we cannot hope to remove them by such means as filling in the holes with some sort of filler material, or by such a process as is used in reweaving, we can often take steps that will minimize the effect of these faults on our copy negative and thus obtain a better copy.

Rejoining the Broken Picture

First, let us consider the extreme case of the picture that has been torn or broken in two or more pieces. It goes without saying that this has to be pieced together before copying. It is important that you be very careful to see that the pieces fit properly. This is most essential when the break passes through the face or part of the body. If the pieces do not fit exactly, a fault will show up on the copy and on the workprint that can result in distortion. You can find yourself with one eye higher than the other, with a change in the line of the lips, or with the nose off center. If the break runs horizontally through the face and the fitting is incorrect, the resulting face can be longer or shorter than it should be. If the break runs vertically, the result can be a wider or narrower face.

There may be a case where you have an original that has been pieced together by someone else. If this is so, you must check the original to make sure that the repiecing is as perfect as it possibly could be. If it is not and if the parts do not match, you should take the picture apart and put it together again properly.

The torn photo can be repieced with the aid of celluloid tape. The tape must be applied to the back of the picture, never to the picture surface. If it is put upon the surface, it will show prominently on the copy. The edges of the tape will reproduce as black lines while the area covered by the transparent tape will be darker than the rest of the picture. The tape may also pick up some glare. And, should you ever try to lift the tape from the surface of the original, it will most likely take off the portion of the emulsion that it covers.

The original that has been rejoined with the aid of celluloid tape may not be flat. If it is a double-weight print, the pieces may have curled and the tape cannot overcome this. To flatten the print so that a good copy can be made, it should be mounted on a stiffer cardboard. This can be done by dry mounting or with rubber cement and pressure. The mounting and pressure will flatten the original. Also, the torn edges will be forced together so that less of the break will show on the copy.

When the picture has been torn into many pieces, taping is impractical. The pieces should be mounted on a cardboard. It is best to use rubber cement, first applying it to the back of the piece, then pressing it on to the board. As the cement does not dry on contact, it gives you time to slide the pieces on the card so they can be fitted together. Before doing this, you should have laid the pieces out to form the picture and to see where each piece goes. This is much like doing a jigsaw puzzle. When the pieces are mounted on the board and properly joined, the print should be under pressure so that the pieces will be flat on the mount and the joinings will not curl up and form ridges.

Curled or Rolled Originals

Many old pictures buckle and curl with age, especially if on single- or double-weight stock and not mounted or framed. Some are kept rolled up into a cylinder and, when they are straightened out for copying, they belly out in the middle and cannot be kept flat. Obviously, these originals have to be perfectly flat to be copied without distortion.

Smaller pictures can most easily be flattened for copying if they can be placed in a printing frame. Since printing frames can be obtained in sizes up to 11″ x 14″, this allows plenty of leeway. All that is required is to place the original in the frame, face against the glass, and cover it with the pressure back. The glass, of course, must be absolutely clean, as you will have to copy through it and do not want to pick up any dirt from it. The use of a nonglare type of glass will prevent any reflections in the glass from the copy lights.

A curled or buckled print can be mounted on a flat cardboard, either with rubber cement under pressure or by dry mounting. This will flatten it and provide a straightened print for the copy camera, eliminating any possible distortion. If the print requires cleaning, it can be better accomplished if it is mounted and flattened. Once the original is mounted, you should not try to remove it from the card after copying or after completing the restoration job. This could cause more damage. Another advantage to mounting in this case is that it is much more handy for the artist to hold the original on his easel when doing the positive retouching and air-brush work, as he uses it for a guide and for comparison with his work on the workprint. Not having to contend with the buckling and curling of the original can save much time.

Occasionally, a previously mounted original will not be straight. It may be curled or buckled. If small enough, it can be placed in a printing frame for copying. If not, you should first attempt to flatten the original by placing it beneath heavy weights. If this does not work, you should moisten the back of the mount and place the picture under pressure again. Allow three or four hours for the pressure to have some effect. If this does not do the trick, you can mount the picture, cardboard backing and all, on a stiffer board. Dry mounting will not work unless the original mount is a thin one, so you should use glue or cement and place the picture under pressure until it dries.

Removing a Print That Is Stuck to Broken Glass

Sometimes you will come across an original that is stuck to a sheet of glass. This may have been done deliberately. With some it has happened because of the glass being damp from cleaning prior to framing, humid atmospheric conditions, or the print not being perfectly dry before framing.

If the sheet of glass is whole and perfect, all you have to do is copy through it. But if the glass is cracked or broken, then you are faced with difficulties. If you copy it as it is, the cracks will show as black lines on the copy. These are extremely difficult to retouch out, especially if the crack passes over some vital facial feature. Therefore, when the glass is cracked, it becomes essential to remove it from the picture.

But this must be accomplished without tearing the emulsion that is bonded to the glass. The only way to do this is by soaking the picture and glass in a tray of water. (However, before doing so, it is a good idea to make an insurance copy negative, just in case.) The original, with the glass on bottom, should be left in the water until, if you are lucky, the print separates itself from the glass and floats up. It will more than likely be necessary to aid the process of separation by pulling the print away from the glass. This should be attempted only when, after an appreciable length of soaking time, the print has not separated itself. The lifting must be done very slowly and cautiously to avoid ripping off any emulsion. If a piece seems to stick, stop working and let the picture soak for another half hour, then try again.

When the entire print is clear of the glass, it should be placed face up on an absorbent cardboard or stiff blotter. Excessive water should be removed by gentle patting with a soft blotter or absorbent cotton. Do not rub! This will only act to slough off the emulsion. Once the water is removed, blotting paper should be placed over the print and it should be allowed to dry with a slight weight on top of it to prevent curling.

24. (LEFT) *A badly cracked photograph.*

25. (RIGHT) *Improvement obtained by copying original in printing frame to lessen the spreading effect of the crack.*

Often when the glass is cracked, the crack is also in the print itself. If this is the case, the picture can come apart along the line of the crack when it is being removed from the glass. This will necessitate careful rejoining. If done correctly, the resulting line will be much less noticeable than if the picture had not been removed from the broken covering glass.

Reducing the Effect of Cracks

Cracks may be minor ones that affect only the emulsion layer of the print or they may be deeper and affect the paper base of the original or even the cardboard backing if it is mounted. These cracks act to form a sort of ridge upon the surface of the picture. There is often an eruption of the emulsion, a separation, and the exposure of the white base beneath. This shows up on the copy as a white line.

A similar effect takes place near the edge of a tear in the print or where it is broken. Pieces of the emulsion stand away and reveal either the white of the paper or the color of the cardboard mount. When copied, these will show up not only as white lines or spots, but will also throw a shadow that will create a black spot or line.

If we can press down these standing pieces of emulsion so they are forced flat against the backing of the picture, these breaks or cracks will not copy as noticeably as if we had copied without such treatment. This can be easily done by placing the original in a printing frame and copying through the glass. The spring back will force the print against the glass. This procedure often eliminates the finer cracks entirely; it minimizes the effects of the more prominent ones.

The printing frame can only be used if the picture will fit into it. If not, or if you have no printing frame, the alternative is to mount the print on a stiff card, either by dry mounting or using rubber cement and pressure. Mounting will not always catch and fasten down the ridges or the loose edges of the broken emulsion. It will flatten most of the print and be an improvement over the untreated print. If the emulsion sticks up after mounting, you can, if you are careful, apply a minute amount of cement right under the upright piece and press it down with your finger until it catches and holds. The cement must not carry over on to the face of the emulsion or it may be ripped off when you remove your finger.

26. (LEFT) A torn photograph with a hole in it.

27. (RIGHT) Improvement obtained by placing gray cards behind the hole to blend closer to the surrounding print area.

Holes

Many damaged prints have holes in them. They usually go through the paper backing. It may seem, at first, that there is nothing we can do about them as far as pre-copy treatment is concerned. It is true that we cannot fill in the hole with filler material or replace the missing piece of the picture. But we can take some simple steps to minimize the fault. This involves backing the hole with a piece of paper or thin cardboard that matches the color or tone of the picture area surrounding it. If an area that consists of black clothing is pierced, then a black backing should be used. If the surrounding area is gray, then we should try to find a matching gray backing. If the hole is in a white shirt or a white dress, then, of course, a white backing should be used. This will not eliminate the fault entirely. The fact that the blemish exists on the original will be revealed on the copy. The edges will photograph as a ring or like the rim of a crater when viewed from above. But this treatment can eliminate much work for the retoucher in later steps of the restoration process.

Of course, the area that surrounds a hole, especially if it is a large one, will not always be of one tone. More than likely, black will blend into gray or white. You may effect a compromise by using a backing that matches the predominant tone or one that is in between the various tones present. You can use some charcoal or white chalk on the backing to darken or lighten it and blend it into the surrounding areas. This will be feasible only if there is enough room for you to work in; if the hole is too small or if too much enlargement is going to be required, the result may be rough and require more retouching.

You should think ahead to the retouching steps and decide whether you will retouch such a hole on the copy negative or on the workprint. If you intend to work on the negative, a darker backing will leave a thinner area on the negative that can be filled in and blended by a retouch pencil. If you are going to use the workprint, then a lighter backing will produce a lighter area that can be blended in with a pencil, tortillon stump, or air brush. This will be easier than the use of an opaque white or gray over a darker spot.

GRAIN

What do we mean by grain? How does it affect restoration work? There are two types of grain that concern us. One is caused by the minute particles of silver grain that combine to form the photographic

28. (ABOVE) Portion of a damaged photograph on silk surfaced paper, showing the effect of texture grain on copying.

29. (BELOW) Improvement obtained by treating the original with a matte spray before copying.

image. Such grain is more apparent in some pictures than in others and is due to variances in exposure, development, and contrast. This is very noticeable when a small picture is enlarged many times or when a small part of a larger picture is cropped out and brought up to a great enlargement. Such grain is an integral part of the picture and cannot be minimized or eliminated by any pre-copy treatment. It has to be handled later on by retouching or airbrushing.

The other type of grain is caused by the rough texture of the paper surface of the original photograph. Print surfaces vary. Some are smooth and even, others are manufactured with special rough or grained finishes. Some have a pebble effect. Some, like silk paper, have a series of fine dots standing up from the paper. Tapestry surfaces are made to resemble an artist's canvas. Linen surfaces resemble the material after which it is named. The patterns of these various surfaces will be picked up by the copy lights and recorded on the copy negative, often obscuring the picture image. Since we want to obtain a copy of the picture, not the texture effect, this grain must be overcome. Whenever possible, it should be done by pre-copy treatment, or by a special procedure while copying. Otherwise, the grain will present a formidable and time-consuming retouching job.

Why Grain Copies

If we examine the grain on the print surface, we will notice that it is made up of a series of high and low points, hills and valleys. This is true, whatever the texture of the grain. The copy lights will tend to throw the shadows of the hills into the valleys. The low parts will be darker than the high ones. This will emphasize the grain. If the paper has any sort of sheen or gloss, some light will bounce off the high spots and be copied as glare. The object, therefore, of any kind of pre-copy treatment of the textured original should be to create, as far as possible, a flat and non-reflecting surface to present to the copy camera.

The Use of a Matte Spray

One way to do this is very simple, easy to accomplish, and works well with originals that have a shallow grain, such as pebble or silk, that are not too large in size, or on which only a small area is to be copied. This involves the use of a commercial, clear, matte or dulling lacquer that comes in compressed air-spray cans. They can be obtained at any art or photo store. The lacquer is applied to the grained surface of the picture. If we are copying the entire picture, then we should spray the entire area. If we are only copying a portion of it, then it is only necessary to cover that particular area. The matte spray will cut down the glare that is thrown off from the high ridges, so that it is not picked up in copying. If enough of the spray solution is applied, it will tend to collect and fill in the valleys, to some extent, so that there is less chance of any shadows falling there.

When spraying the original, it is best to have the original lying horizontally and to hold the spray can at least eighteen inches away. Do not apply the spray too rapidly or liquid drops will form. Instructions are on the can, both for using the solution and for removing it afterwards, should that be desirable. Of course, the original should be cleaned before the application of the spray lacquer.

The Use of Petroleum Jelly

The method just described depends mostly upon its dulling effects to kill the grain. We can also try to fill in the low spots or valleys, so that a flat surface is created and the grain lost. This involves the use of some clear substance that can be applied to the surface, will fill the valleys, and will not obscure the image.

One material that we can use is petroleum jelly. It proves very effective with smaller originals, but it is not practical to use it on larger ones. The jelly is applied and rubbed on to the print surface. The use of the fingers is best. This gives you the best control in applying the jelly, since you can put it where you want and in the amounts you want. Cotton or cloth can be used, but when they are, some lint can stick to the print and be picked up in the copy, thus creating more work for the retoucher. The jelly can be applied lightly, and there is no need to rub it in hard. Enough should be used to fill the valleys and cover the print. When this is done, the original should be placed into a printing frame, preferably one with a nonglare glass. The pressure of the spring back will force the jelly into the valleys, while the ridges are pressed against the glass. This presents a flat surface to the copy camera and no grain should be photographed. Of course, this is a little messy. The petroleum jelly must be removed from the print after you finish copying it, and the glass will have to be cleaned each time you use this method. But, if you get rid of the grain, it is worth it.

The Use of Shellac

Another material that can be used is clear white shellac. As far as filling in the valleys is concerned, the shellac will have the same effect as

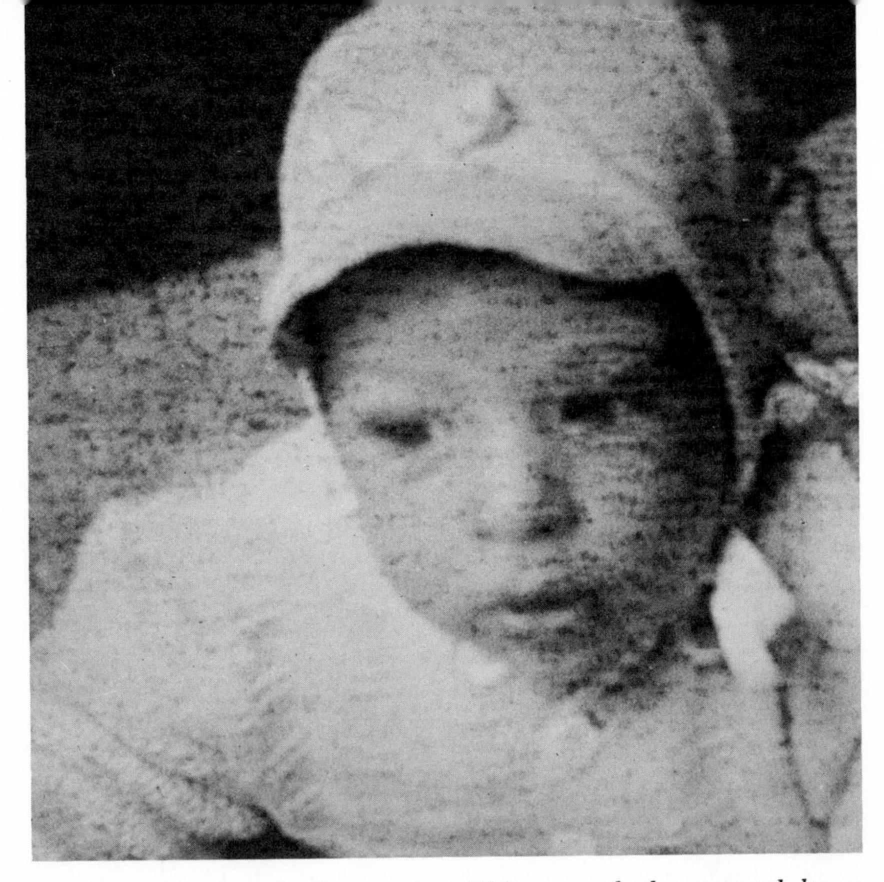

30. Chemical grain in the negative. This can only be removed by retouching.

petroleum jelly. But, shellac dries on the print and is difficult to remove. In fact, whenever possible, you should not attempt to remove it. The fact that it does dry on the print is an advantage, inasmuch as the print is easier to handle and no printing frame is needed.

One method of applying the shellac is to pour it over the print and allow it to spread. The print has to be lying flat. The shellac is poured over it slowly and is permitted to flow over the entire surface of the print. It is a good idea to do this in an old photo tray, so you can move or agitate it and help the spread of the shellac solution. If the shellac seems to be too thick, it can be thinned down with denatured alcohol. However, if it is made too thin, the method will not work, for after drying, the grain will remain. This method can only work if the shellac is of the proper thickness. This is something you will have to learn with use and experience. You should first experiment with some expendable prints to get the knack of the process. The print should be left alone until the shellac is dry. Cover the tray so no dust can fall on the wet shellac. When dry, the shellac should form a flat, clear layer in which the grain has disappeared.

This pouring method will work on smaller prints, but becomes impractical for larger size prints. On originals that are larger than 8″ x 10″, it is better to apply the shellac by brush. The brush should be at least an inch and a half in width and of a very fine bristle. While the shellac must be thick enough to fill in the valleys and form a layer with a flat surface, it must not be so thick that it retains the streaks of the brush, nor should it be so thin that, upon drying, the grain remains. Here, too, trial and error with an expendable print will be helpful until you get the knack of this technique. The original should be in a horizontal position while being shellacked and dried.

The shellac can also be applied by spraying. However, your regular air brush cannot be used. A larger spray gun or paint sprayer is required. The thickness of your spraying solution must be determined by use, as with the two methods just described. Practice prints should be used until you get the knack of spraying. The print should be flat and the shellac sprayed on so that a layer builds up, drowning the grain. Do not hold the gun too close to the pictures, or the shellac will build up into waves and streak or run. Keep it at least three feet away. When you feel the print has been properly covered with the shellac, it should be allowed to dry protected from dust.

The shellac will leave a glossy finish on the original, which can be reflected by the copy lights and cause glare, unless these lights are set up properly. This will be discussed in the chapter on copying.

Eliminating Grain on Damaged Originals

If the original is cracked or torn, or if the emulsion is lifting up in places, it may not be advisable to attempt to eliminate the grain by pre-copy work, if doing so will damage the original to a greater extent. Of course, such treatment as already described, cleaning and mounting, should have been accomplished before this. Now, we should examine the grain or texture and decide what should be done about it.

If we feel that the application of the matte spray from the compressed can of gas can kill the grain, this can be done. Since there will be no rubbing or pressure applied to the surface of the original and since nothing

31. (LEFT) *A daguerreotype in its case.*

32. (RIGHT) *Improvement obtained by removal from the case and elimination of the dirty covering glass before copying.*

will be done that can damage or pull at the torn emulsion, we can use this method safely.

The application of petroleum jelly involves rubbing over the surface of the original and the risk of tearing up a piece of emulsion. Also, should this be done without damage, the picture would have to be placed into the printing frame and then removed. There is the chance of the emulsion sticking to the glass and ripping off in this process. Brushing the shellac on the picture can cause pieces of broken emulsion to be picked up by the brush as it passes over the torn areas.

So the question you must ask yourself is, "If I spray this original, if I use petroleum jelly on it, if I shellac it, will the emulsion be removed from the damaged areas?" If you feel that it will, then this treatment must be omitted. You will have to try to reduce the effect of the grain in copying.

SPECIAL PRE-COPY TREATMENT FOR VARIOUS TYPES OF ORIGINALS

Original photographs fall into several classes. These are daguerreotypes, ambrotypes, tintypes, mounted prints, unmounted prints, crayon or pastel enlargements, and hand-colored prints. Also, we can add to these a new source of original material for restoration—natural color prints. The basis for these classifications is solely the manner of handling these originals, especially before copying. It has nothing to do with their age or historical period, the manner in which they were made, or with their photographic quality. Each of these requires different pre-copy treatment and with each there is some type of treatment that should be avoided.

The Daguerreotype

We will begin with a discussion of the daguerreotype, since it is the oldest type of original photograph you can be called on to restore. This picture consists of a photographic image that has been fixed on a silver or copper plate. These small pictures were placed into small cases and covered with glass when presented to the customer. In many instances, when they are presented for restoration, they are still in the same case. As long as the original is encased, it cannot be treated. All you can do is clean the outside surface of the covering glass. To get at the daguerreotype itself, you must remove it from the case.

This is a simple task. When originally placed in the case, the sheet of glass had been placed on top of the metal print. Then a mat of metal

33. (LEFT) *An ambrotype in its case.*

34. (RIGHT) *Improvement obtained by removal from the case and providing a new backing for the ambrotype before copying.*

foil was placed on top and folded under them. This made a unit that was forced into the snugly fitting case and held there by the pressure of the sides. To remove the daguerreotype from the case, this process has to be reversed. A razor blade or the point of a thin penknife is forced between the glass and the edge of the case and used as a lever to pry out the daguerreotype and glass. Once this is done, the mat can be removed by simply unfolding it. This is easily done by hand, and no tool is necessary. Then the daguerreotype is separated from the glass. It should separate easily and should not stick to the glass. Should it stick, however, proceed no further. Just clean the face of the glass and make your copy through it.

The main reason for removing the print from the case is to eliminate the piece of glass, which may be so dirty or pitted from age that it cannot be cleaned perfectly. A better copy can be obtained without it. We can assume that since it has been protecting the daguerreotype, there is no dirt layer present and cleaning is not required. If there are stains or marks, they are of a chemical nature. These usually are bluish in tone and give the impression that the picture has been scorched by the flame of a match. Do not attempt to rub them off. It is very important to remember that the surface of a daugerreotype should never be rubbed with a dry cloth, a moistened cloth, or by your hand! One peculiarity of this type of photograph is that rubbing the surface will weaken the image and may remove it entirely. Therefore, even if you feel the stain could be eliminated, even if it covers a very vital area of the picture, do not attempt to remove it. Should there be dust on the surface, blow it off. Do not brush it.

Some daguerreotypes, because they have been made on a silver plate, reflect light like a mirror and the image is visible only when viewed by holding the picture at a certain angle to the light. Do not make any attempt to overcome this effect. Do not experiment with it. If you attempt to tone down the reflectiveness with a matte spray, the image can disappear. If you attempt to rub it or clean it, the same thing can happen. When this daguerreotype is being copied and the lights are properly positioned, the image will be recorded without any trace of the reflection.

As a general rule, no pre-copy treatment should be done to a daguerreotype except for cleaning the cover glass, removing it from the case, or blowing off any dust.

The Ambrotype

In appearance, the ambrotype resembles the daguerreotype and it is difficult to notice any difference. Both are usually found in the same

35. Tintype. The illustration on the left has been copied without treatment. The one on the right has been coated with petroleum jelly to brighten the image. However, note the streaks created by an uneven application of the jelly on the left of the picture.

type of case. However, the ambrotype is not made on a metal plate, as the daguerreotype is, but on a piece of glass. It can be removed from its case by the same method as was described for the daguerreotype.

The image is found on the emulsion side of the glass plate. This side is covered by a protective glass, while the back is coated with black paint, which brings up the image and makes it visible. Without the coating, all you would see is a thin, negative image when the image is held up to light.

As in the case of the daguerreotype, the image surface is extremely delicate and must not be rubbed or cleaned. While we must be careful with the emulsion side, the back of the glass plate can be worked on if necessary. It can be worked on when the paint backing has flaked off, which is common with this type of original photograph. Where this has happened, the image seems to have disappeared and there is an apparent hole in the picture. However, this can be made to reappear by repainting the back and covering the flaked spots with black tempera, water color, or any quick-drying, black paint.

Since the image has been protected by the glass, there should be no layer of dirt accumulated on it. Should there be any dust or loose dirt, it should be removed by blowing, either by mouth or air brush.

Whenever possible, the ambrotype should be removed from its case for copying, so that it is not necessary to copy through the protective glass, which may be stained or pitted with age. But, as with the daguerreotype, if the glass does not separate easily from the ambrotype, leave it alone. Copy through the glass.

The main thing to remember about pre-copy work with ambrotypes is not to touch or handle the picture surface (the emulsion side of the glass). But the back of the glass can be repainted or touched up to fill in holes due to the flaking off of the old backing.

The Tintype

Tintypes are direct positive pictures. They are not found in cases, as are the daguerreotype and ambrotype, though many of them date from the same time. Here the sensitized photographic emulsion was placed upon a thin sheet of steel, or "tin." This is the reason for the name "tintype." In more recent years, thick paper or thin cardboard was used as a base instead of metal, but the name remained. Such pictures were made, especially by sidewalk photographers, as late as 1950.

The most apparent fault with this type of original photograph is its darkness. There are no whites. Those areas that should be white are gray and the middle tones are almost black. The image is flat, dark, and obscure and shows itself only in strong light. This image should somehow be brought out so that it can be photographed.

The tintype image is not as delicate as that of the daguerreotype or the ambrotype. It can be treated and handled. We can touch and rub it, something we dared not do with the other two types. If dirt is present, it may be removed by cleaning. Since most tintypes have not been protected by a case, there is a good possibility of a dirt layer being present.

With few exceptions, the image on the daguerreotypes is a dull one; it needs to be brightened. If we put a drop of water on it, the spot covered by the water becomes more brilliant and the picture is not harmed.

36. A tintype with a pitted surface. This original cannot be treated. Artwork and retouching are the only means for restoration.

However, the use of water is impractical since it evaporates quickly and the effect is lost. The tintype can be immersed in a tray of water only if it is on a steel plate. This is about the only type of original with which this can be done. This will brighten the image but requires a special vertical copy set-up, which may be impractical for you.

Here we can find petroleum jelly very useful. It brings out the image, as does water, but does not evaporate. It should be applied sparingly and rubbed in with care so that no streaks form that catch light and cause white lines on the copy. Fingers are the best means of application, as cotton or cloth can leave lint on the picture.

Shellac can produce the same effect. It can be sprayed on in a solution diluted with denatured alcohol, so that it can go through the air brush. It can be applied with a fine brush. Care must be taken that no dust falls on the picture while the shellac is drying. Then you must never attempt to remove the shellac with any medium or you might remove the emulsion.

This treatment, while it will make the image seem to be more visible, will not lighten it or increase the contrast. This is something that has to be done when copying and making the workprint. At the very least, it will make the image more visible and therefore easier to focus upon when copying. This alone is worth the effort.

Sometimes you will come across a tintype that is pitted, with pieces of emulsion missing and rusted metal showing through. However, this will not prevent your treating the picture with petroleum jelly or shellac to brighten the image. Careful application will not cause the remaining emulsion to peal off in this case. But there is no way to fill in these spots or reduce their effect in this step. They will show up on the copy and have to be removed by retouching.

The tintype may be bent or undulated. If the curvature affects the facial area, distortion in copying can result. The tintype should be placed in a press and the pressure applied slowly until the metal base is flattened. This should be done prior to any treatment for brightening the image with petroleum jelly or shellac.

Mounted Originals

Whether the mounted original is an old or recent one, we may find physical damage to the mount and both physical and chemical damage to the print itself. If the damage to the mount lies outside the picture area, it can be ignored. But if the mount is damaged where it backs the print, we must pay attention to it.

What can we expect to find wrong with the mount? It can be broken, cracked, or crumbled. This is important since it can affect the surface of the print we want to copy. Any attempt to remove the print from the mount is out of the question. This would require soaking the print and the mount, which will cause more damage or even complete disintegration.

When the mount is broken or in separate pieces, the picture will also be broken. In piecing this together, use either friction tape on the

37. Typical crayon enlargement attached to copy board with pushpins.

back of the mount, never on the front over the picture, or remount both picture and mount on a solid board. If the mount is cracked and not flat, it should be remounted. This should be done under pressure so that it will also flatten the picture and minimize the cracks.

These prints usually require cleaning. Since the mount has been allowed to deteriorate, it is only reasonable to assume that no effort had been made to protect the actual picture and that a layer of dirt or grime is present. This cleaning should not be started until you have fixed the mount and have a more solid surface on which to work.

Unmounted Originals

As in the case of the mounted original, an unmounted one can be an old or more recent print and can be broken, torn, cracked, and in need of cleaning.

If torn or broken, it can be mended by the use of friction tape on the back of the print, never on the face. Wherever possible, this print should be mounted upon a stiff cardboard, either by dry mounting or by the use of rubber cement and pressure. This will serve to flatten the print, subdue the cracks, and provide a more solid surface for cleaning and copying. If for any reason you cannot, or do not want to, mount the print, place it in a printing frame for copying, and it will flatten out.

When the picture is cracked or buckled, it can be straightened by mounting under pressure or by being placed in a printing frame for copying.

Crayon or Pastel Enlargements

There are enlargements in existence that were made in large numbers during the decades preceding and following World War I. These pictures were either stretched on a frame or stretcher, much as an oil painting, or pressed into a convex mount and trimmed to an oval shape. Most were finished in color by pastel or air brush. Others were finished in black and white or sepia by crayon or air brush. Almost all of these prints have some degree of artwork on them. It is important to recognize this.

In many instances, the photographic image itself has faded. The artwork is all that is left of the picture. This is a peculiarity of this type of original photograph. Where the artwork has been applied heavily, completely covering and building up the original photograph, the loss of the underlying photographic image is not noticeable. However, should this artwork be removed or rubbed off during cleaning, there may be no picture left to copy.

When we come across one of these originals mounted on a stretcher, we will often find that the picture is coming off the stretcher, that it is pierced and torn, or that the photoprint is separating from the cloth backing. In such circumstances, it is advisable to remove the picture from the stretcher entirely and remount it. It should be dry mounted on a stiff cardboard. Do not use wet paste, liquid cement, or rubber cement. Those substances can cause new stains to appear by attacking the picture from the back of the print.

Those prints that have been trimmed to oval shape and pressed ino a convex form present other problems. The cardboard backing is usually thin and brittle and it is often cracked and broken. If at any time pressure had been applied to the surface of the picture, it would have caused a crack to travel from the edge to the center of the print. This crack usually passes through the figure or face of the subject. Because of the convex shape of the print, this crack separates and widens. The edges of the crack must be forced together and joined by applying strong plastic or adhesive tape to the back. Transparent tape should not be applied to the surface, for it will show up in the copy and will pull the emulsion from the print, if you should have to remove it.

Never try to flatten the convex print. You may be tempted to do so in order to create a level surface for copying, but all you will do is crack and break it.

Once repairs have been made to the mounting and the picture is on a solid foundation, we can look at it. Since the prints have almost always been finished by air brush, water, or pastel colors, any water or cleaning solution applied to them will only cause further damage. It will remove or streak the old artwork. Some of these prints may have been varnished or shellacked. Often the varnish has become lined with fine cracks that show up in the copying. Should you try to remove the varnish with turpentine or another solvent? No. You may remove more than the varnish; you may remove the picture itself. Revarnishing might help. It will subdue the fine cracks in the old varnish. If you do try this, the varnish should be applied by an air brush or spray can, not by a hand brush.

The main thing we can accomplish with this type of original is to strengthen or fix the mount or backing. The picture surface is usually too fragile to permit any type of cleaning.

However, if the mount and picture surface are in good, although not necessarily perfect, condition and the picture is faded or has some scratches that are not deep, the air brush or pastels can be used to recolor and build up the picture. New color can be applied to freshen the old. As long as the surface is clean, it will accept new work. The medium used has to be compatible, however, to the original medium. Pastel will be acceptable to a pastel print, air-brush water color to an air-brushed print. Transparent oil colors will not work on them. If the print had been varnished, it is very improbable that any medium would be usable.

When you have a convex original in which the mount is in good shape and you wish to retain the same shape or use the same frame, it is often better to freshen the original than to make a copy restoration. It is difficult to duplicate the convex shape, as prints of this type have gone out of style and are not produced commercially any longer. Also, in copying a convex print, a slight amount of distortion occurs, which, unfortunately, cannot be avoided. You are actually restoring the old photograph and this is about the only type of original with which you can do this.

Hand-Colored Originals

The hand-colored prints classified here are usually professional studio type photos made from the period of the 1920s to date. These have been colored or tinted by air brush, water colors, aniline dyes, or transparent oils. Cleaning such prints is difficult because it can remove the coloring. It becomes necessary, therefore, to determine just how the print had been colored. An experienced restorer can tell this by merely looking at the originals. However, there are some simple tests which you can do.

A water-based cleaner, such as the liquid soap solution or diluted ammonia we mentioned earlier, will remove the coloring if it is airbrush or water color. Rubbing with an eraser will also remove this type of coloring and will remove transparent oil coloring as well. Only the aniline dyes will survive cleaning.

A dirt layer can affect a colored print just as well as a black-and-white print. So, if the coloring is stained, soiled, or damaged, removing it will more than likely give you a much cleaner print to copy. If it does, then it is worthwhile to remove the coloring.

You can test the coloring by touching the corner of the print with a swab of cotton. If the cotton is dipped in water and the color comes off on it readily, the print was airbrushed or water colored. If the water does not do this, but spirits of turpentine do, then it was oil colored. If neither of these remove the coloring, we can assume that aniline dyes were used.

But the object is not to remove the coloring. If the print had been water colored, the cleaning solution will remove the coloring. We cannot help that. But, if it had been oil colored, the cleaning solution should only remove the dirt, not the color. Of course, the cleaning must be done carefully and delicately. If the print is rubbed too hard, the oil coloring can be removed by the action of the rubbing.

The print may have been varnished or shellacked. If so, the coloring is protected. Any dirt would be on top of the layer of varnish. Cleaning should remove it without disturbing the color beneath.

When the colored print has been made on a grained or textured surface, another problem arises quite often. The color tends to collect in the deeper holes of the texturing and is deeper or heavier in those spots.

This negates any attempt to eliminate that texture, either by pre-copy work or in copying. These heavier spots of color not only increase the effect of the grain but show up as black spots on the copy print. In such cases, removal of the coloring is necessary. If water color or air brush, it can be removed by using a moist swab of cotton; if oil, by the use of cotton dipped in spirits of turpentine.

If the print is cracked, torn, or broken, it should be joined or mounted as we have described earlier. This should be done before cleaning or removing the color. It is always possible to recolor the print after cleaning and removing the original coloring. The result may not be perfect; that is, as perfect as it would be if you were coloring a fresh print. The colors may not take as well. But, if you think recoloring necessary, the results will probably be equal to or better than the original with the dirt. The perfect results will be sought in the restored print.

Natural Color Prints

We make special mention of natural color prints, even though, for the most part, pre-copy treatment would be the same as for any unmounted photographic print. More of this type of work, both professional and amateur, is being done, and as time goes on, some of this will be presented to the photo-restorer for copying and restoration.

These originals may be torn, cracked, or covered with a layer of dirt and grime. If torn or cracked, they should be rejoined by the use of adhesive tape on the back of the print, never on the face. If you want to mount them, this should be done by dry mounting. Cement or paste can be absorbed by the paper and affect the image, change color values, or cause stains.

A layer of dirt should be removed only by the use of a cotton swab moistened with the liquid soap solution. Do not try to rub the dirt off with an eraser. The emulsion on color prints is very sensitive to such rubbing and is easily scratched. Do not use a solution of ammonia.

When water touches some color prints, the area affected by the wetting turns blue. This is a temporary condition. As soon as the water has dried or evaporated, the natural color returns.

Some color prints, usually professional ones, have been textured. This texture has usually been pressed into the emulsion by a machine, but the effect, as far as copying is concerned, is the same. Such texture can be treated with matte spray, as we have described earlier. Petroleum jelly and copying in a printing frame can be used when the print is small enough to fit into the frame. Shellac will work, but cannot be removed.

The purpose of all pre-copy preparation is to improve the condition of the original picture as much as possible and to correct and overcome whatever faults we can, so that we can eliminate much retouching and restoration that may be required later. Such pre-copy work consists, for the most part, of making repairs to the physical condition of the original photograph. We do this by repiecing, remounting, rejoining, cleaning, and removing dirt.

When you do this, you should use practical common sense. If you do so and exercise caution, you should improve the original, not make it worse.

CHAPTER 3

COPYING

Copying the original photograph is not a simple matter of placing it in front of some camera and snapping the shutter. The equipment you use for copying differs in many respects from that used for regular photographic work. Special equipment for copying is not essential. You can get some sort of copy negative with any camera. But "some sort" of copy negative is not good enough. There are certain qualities we want our copy negative to have.

First, the copy negative must be large enough to be worked on. This will eliminate miniature and subminiature sizes, as well as the popular 120 roll film sizes. They are used for copying, it is true, but as far as restoration work is concerned, they are too small.

Secondly, you should have a substantial base supporting the film so that it will be easier to work on. Roll film and film packs are too thin for this purpose. Cut film is the best for our purpose. The smallest size advisable is 3¼"x4¼".

The image on the copy negative should be as large as possible. It is of little value to use a cut film of proper size while the working image is small. When working with a small original, it should be enlarged as much as possible in the copying. When taking out part of an original for work, this section should be cropped to proper proportions on the copy negative. The larger the image on the copy negative, the easier it will be to work on and the better the final results will be. This requires the use of a view camera with a long bellows of double or triple extension for copying.

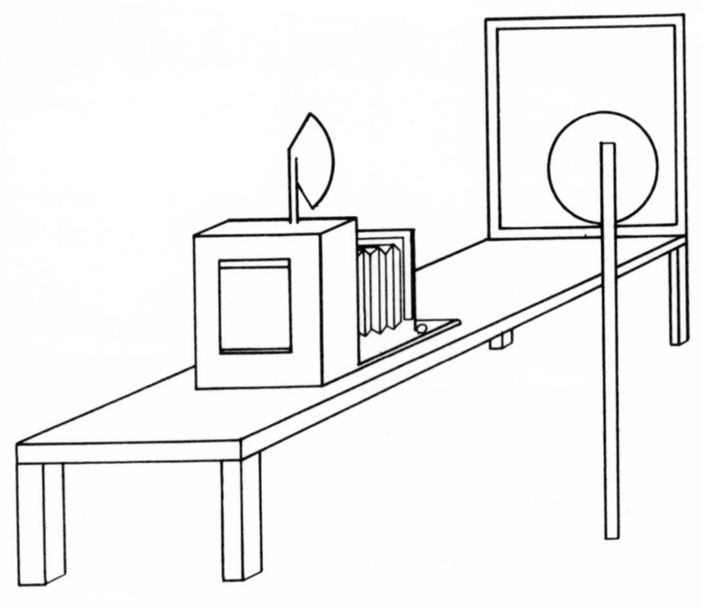

38. Typical copying setup.

In copying, the material being photographed must be absolutely parallel to the film. Otherwise, some distortion will result. This means the camera must be fixed at right angles, both vertically and horizontally, to the copyboard. If possible, this should be a permanent set-up.

Even illumination is necessary so that one portion of the original photograph does not receive more or less light than another. Here, too, a permanent set-up is advisable, so the lights do not have to be adjusted each time you have to make a copy negative.

Let's see what we need. First, we want a good copy camera of the view type with a long bellows extension. Then we want a permanent copyboard and some sort of track or support for our camera that will be perpendicular to the copyboard. And third, we want a set of copy lights to provide proper illumination of the material we want to copy. This will provide your basic set-up of camera, copyboard, and lights.

You can purchase complete copying outfits, or you can set up your own. It is not the purpose of this book to tell you what to do in this respect. We will just present the basics and the theory as they relate to copying photographs for the purpose of photo-restoration only!

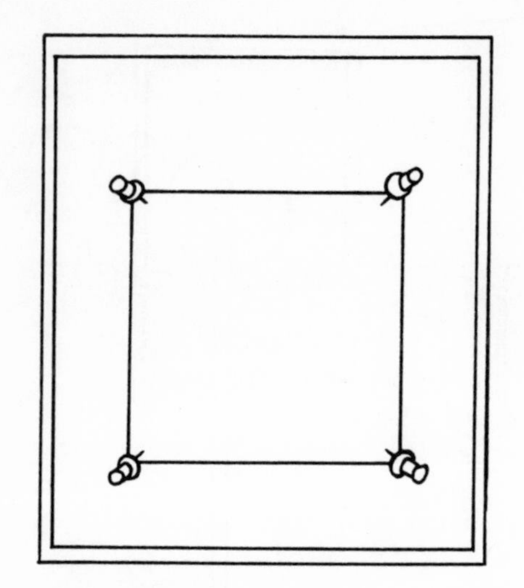

39. Method of attaching work to copyboard with pushpins.

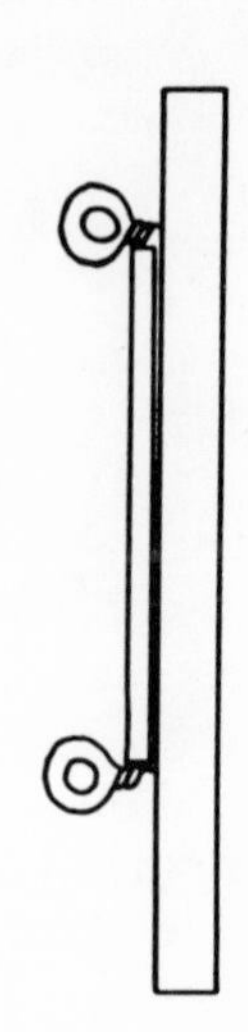

40. Method of holding work on copyboard with screw eyes.

41. (BELOW) Vertical copying setup.

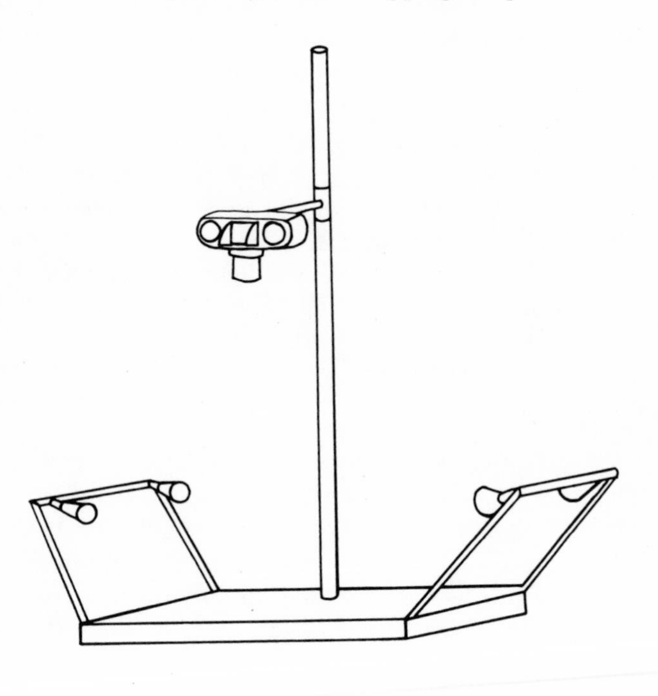

Photo-copying and reproduction are used extensively in graphic arts, commercial photography, etc., but this is not our province. If you are interested in these aspects of copying, there are other books that deal primarily and extensively with this subject.

SETTING UP A BASIC COPY ARRANGEMENT

If you want to make up the basic copying set-up yourself, you can start by obtaining a copyboard or some permanent surface to hold the original pictures being copied. A simple solution would be to obtain a cork bulletin board and attach it firmly to a wall. The wall itself, if perfectly flat, can be used, but it would be difficult to hold the work on the wall. With the bulletin board, the pictures can be held on by thumbtacks or pushpins.

The bulletin board should be bracketed with lights to provide illumination. The simplest solution is to use two reflectors with 150-watt bulbs. They should be placed equidistant from the center line of the copyboard and at the same distance from the wall. If you have the reflectors on movable stands, a mark can be made on the floor to show where the stands should be placed. You can attach the reflectors to the copyboard with some sort of an arm arrangement. You can also attach them to the camera support. It is not necessary to use photofloods. Bulbs smaller than 150 watts can also be used. It will just mean a longer exposure. But since you are not dealing with moving subjects, this is not important.

Your next step is to provide some sort of support or track, perpendicular to the copyboard, on which to place the copy camera. A long, narrow table or a plank mounted on sawhorses can be easily used. The table or board must be tracked so the camera can be moved forward or back as required and still remain perpendicular to the copyboard. Such a track, or guide, can be made by taking two pieces of moulding and attaching them to the table, parallel to each other and separated by the width of the camera bed. This should provide a snug fit so that, while you can move the camera, it will not pop out of the tracks.

You have a wide choice when it comes to obtaining a view camera to use for the copying. The method just described has been suggested to allow you to adapt any press or view camera you might have, and thus avoid the expense of buying a special camera. At the same time, when the camera is not being used for copying, it can be used for other work. When needed for copy work, all you have to do is set it in the track.

Examine the accompanying illustration, which shows the basic copy arrangement. It can be varied to accommodate the use of different types of cameras, lights, tables, or copyboards. Thus you can adapt equipment that you have in your possession or that you can obtain easily and inexpensively. But whatever equipment you use, wherever you set it up, it will follow this pattern.

USING THE COPYBOARD

Work can be attached to the copyboard by pinning it with pushpins. They can be put in and pulled out by hand. Thumbtacks can also be used, but would require the use of a penknife or blade to remove them from the board. If you use thumbtacks, do not pierce the photo being copied, but allow the head of the tack to hold it to the board.

When an original is curled or frayed at the edges, it should be taped or pasted to a stiffer card, so that you have a flat surface to copy. The picture will be easier to handle and any chance of tearing it further in attaching it to the board will be eliminated. Of course, this is part of the pre-copy treatment. Such an original can also be copied in a printing frame.

Some originals may be mounted on a heavy card that curls at the edges and that the pushpins cannot hold to the copyboard. Or they may be mounted on something too thick for the pushpins. Or the originals may be very large. In such instances you can use screw eyes, placing one near each corner of the picture, at the top and bottom edges. The screw eye is worked into the copyboard just at the edge of the picture, so that when it is into the board as much as possible, its eye is at right angles to the edge of the print and supports it, as well as forcing it flat against the board. Larger screw eyes can be used to provide the support necessary to hold a printing frame to the copyboard. Because of its thickness, pushpins would be useless.

Guidelines

Guidelines can be placed on the copyboard to show you where to pin the work. They can be a time saver. Since the camera track is fixed, the camera should always be on the same line or track, perpendicular to the copyboard, even if you do remove it for other work than copying. If you locate the point on the copyboard that always falls in the center of the view screen of your camera, then two perpendicular lines passing through this point will form two similar lines passing through the center of the viewing screen. This can be refined by outlining standard sizes, such as 4″ x 5″, 5″ x 7″, 8″ x 10″, etc., so that you can readily see where to place the work being copied and that the image will fall properly into place on the view screen without any time-consuming adjustment.

These lines will be of value as an aid in focusing only when the original print is on single- or double-weight stock and unmounted. If it is on a thick card or in a printing frame, it will be closer to the camera than the guidelines, so if you do focus on the guidelines, the image will not be in sharp focus. In such instances, the guidelines might prove confusing. Focusing should be concentrated on the image of the original.

USING THE CAMERA

Focusing

The big advantage afforded by the use of the view camera for copying is the opportunity to use the ground glass back for focusing. The ground glass back enables you to get the sharpest possible copy and to crop or reposition the subject while making the negative. Since you see what you are doing, you can also adjust or vary the size of the image on the copy negative to match that of another negative. This can be important, as we will show later, in combining subjects from separate originals onto one photo. If your originals are attached to the copyboard in an upside-down position, they will show right side up on the ground glass. It is easier to judge and focus in this position.

If the image being copied is sharp, there should be no difficulty in obtaining a sharp image on the viewing screen. But if the image is not sharp and if it is diffused or out of focus, the best we can hope for is an image of equivalent sharpness. It is not easy to determine by observation if such an image is in proper focus since there are no sharp lines to guide you.

Should the original be a snapshot with a masked edge or any print with a border defined by a sharp line, this can be used as a guide. Concentrate or focus on it. When it is at its sharpest on the ground glass, the rest of the picture must also be at its sharpest. If, due to cropping or some other reason, the border does not fall on the negative, just move the original on the copyboard so that the line does fall on the ground glass. Then, when the focusing is completed, move it back to the proper position. Since the camera and the copyboard are fixed, this should not disturb the focusing.

If there is no sharp line on the original, make one. Cover half of the original with a piece of thin, stiff paper or a business card and concentrate on the edge. The same thing can be done with a piece of masking tape. However, if you use tape, be sure that it will not cause any damage to the original when it is removed. You also may use a fine spotting brush, with black or white water color, depending upon the original, to paint a sharp line on or near the edge of the print that can be your guide. If you do this, it should be on some part of the original that you intend to crop out of the copy. Do not apply this to any important area. If you do, you would have to wash it off before copying and may find some streaks left.

When focusing, the lens should be opened to its widest stop, to allow the brightest possible image to fall on the ground glass. This will, of course, make the focusing easier than if you stopped down the lens and had to view a darker image. Since there is no depth of field or any third dimension of depth to consider, there is actually no reason to stop down the lens for your exposure. But, since you are copying a fixed object and speed of exposure is not important either, you can stop down the lens and increase the exposure time proportionately. Many photographers like to do this as a safety measure, just in case there was a small measure of sharpness they might have missed.

Reducing by Copying

Since you will be using a 4″ x 5″ back and 4″ x 5″ cut film, or a smaller size, you will have to reduce any original that is larger in size. This is done simply by moving the camera away from the copyboard and decreasing the bellows extension while focusing. Here is where you can see the purpose of the track. This insures the proper position of the camera while it is being moved closer to or farther away from the copyboard. It keeps the camera perpendicular at all times to the board.

When the originals are very large, the center mark on the copyboard may not hold true. This will depend upon how the copying set-up is arranged. If it is arranged in the manner we have illustrated, the image of the large original will fall too low on the ground glass screen. This can be overcome by raising the camera back. Most view cameras have a back that can be lowered or raised to accommodate a situation like this. Or, it may be possible to raise the lens board. But, if neither of these is possible for you, you can use a block of wood to lift your camera above the track, so that it becomes centered on the original, instead of the original centering on the camera. You must be sure when you do this that you keep the axis of the camera at right angles to the copyboard.

Enlarging Small Originals in Copying

At the standard bellows extension and distance from the copyboard, small originals will be very tiny on the copy negative. While it will be

42. (ABOVE) *Print from copy negative showing the entire picture image*

43. (BELOW) *Print from copy negative of same original which has been cropped, in copying, to show just the head and shoulder portion of the picture.*

possible to make enlargements from such small images, you will have no chance to do any work such as retouching or blocking on the copy negative, because of the size of the image. And, also, a large degree of magnification would be required which the average enlarging machine might not be able to handle. The same would be true when you want to restore or reproduce a certain part of the original picture, as in the case of taking the head of one subject from a group photo.

Since the copy film size is larger than the original, or desired portion of it, a degree of enlargement obtained while copying is desirable. It is possible to obtain a larger image on the copy negative if the bellows of the camera can be extended far enough. The closer the lens is brought to the work being copied, the longer the bellows has to be in order to get a sharp image on the ground glass and the larger the resulting image. Here is where the double extension bellows of a view camera is valuable.

You should always try to obtain the largest possible image on your copy negative. This will become clear when you try to spot, retouch, or airbrush the negative. It also will be of great help if the magnification range of your enlarger is limited.

FILMS

Since most originals are monochromes, the use of color-corrected high-speed films is not necessary. Orthochromatic films, such as commercial or commercial ortho, should be able to handle most of your restoration copy requirements. These films will tend to pick up contrast, and with the use of a contrasty developer they can pick up even more. This is important when we deal with faded or weak originals. However, when the image is very faint, a process type film should be used.

Colored or painted originals should be copied with panchromatic films, especially when reds or warm tones predominate.

We mentioned the use of cut film. For copying, especially copy for restoration purposes, this is the best type. Above all it is convenient. If you need to make only one copy and need it in a hurry, you can expose and develop it. You do not have to wait to use up the rest of a roll of film or the remainder of a film pack. Loading separate film holders may be some bother, but any such bother is more than overcome by the advantages to the use of the cut film. The advantage becomes obvious when, for example, you have to copy eleven originals that require commercial film and one that requires process or panchromatic film.

The base of the cut film is thicker than that of film packs or roll film. This may not seem to be important, but it does make work easier for the retoucher who wants to spot, block, or airbrush the copy negative. The thicker base makes the negative more workable and easier to handle.

Size of the negative should be considered only as to convenience and cost. The following sizes will fit most standard enlargers and are large enough to be worked on: 4″x5″, 3¼″x4¼″, and, perhaps, 2¼″x3¼″. A 5″x7″ or 8″x10″ copy negative would be ideal for such work, but they are more expensive than the smaller sizes. Then again there are not as many enlarging machines that can accommodate these sizes. While you should be able to do a more detailed retouching job on these, it is doubtful that the slight advantage will be worth the additional expense involved, provided you have the equipment necessary at your command.

FILTERS

Filters can be of value in copying to help eliminate some faults of the original picture that we could not take care of in the pre-copy treatment. These would be certain stains, discolorations, faded or faint images, and texture grains.

If the stain is black, white, very dark, or strong, we cannot hope to remove it by filtering. But, if it is, for example, a light color such as yellow, blue, light brown, or red, or if it is the mark of a rubber stamp, filtering can help. However, the image on the original must be a strong black and white and not faded. Here, panchromatic film must be used. We must choose a filter that is similar in color to the stain; that is, if the stain is yellow, we would use a yellow filter, if blue, a blue filter, and so on. The filter should be deeper in tone than the stain. If we copy the original using panchromatic film and a filter of the same color as the stain, the stain should be eliminated or reduced on the copy negative.

But suppose you have two stains of different colors. You cannot get rid of both on one copy. The attempt to filter out one of the stains may intensify the other one. This makes it necessary for you to decide which of the two stains to eliminate and whether or not the elimination or reduction of one stain warrants the intensification of the other. Does one cause more trouble than the other? Is one in a more important place on the picture? If one is on the face and the other on the background, which one should be filtered out? Which one would be easier to eliminate by airbrushing? Suppose there is a blue mark on the face and a yellow one in the background. If you use the blue filter, the face may become clean but there will be a black spot in the background. It's simpler to airbrush out a black mark from the background, when retouching the workprint, than it is to eliminate a similar mark from the face. Therefore, this should reveal the pattern of choices in these situations. The stain that affects the most important area of the picture is the one on which to work. Which is more important? Well, as a rule, the face is more important than the clothing, the clothing more important than the background, and the center of the picture more important than the edges.

With a faded original, our main concern at this time is to build up the contrast. So if we have a faded print that is also stained, building up the contrast is of more importance to us than getting rid of the stain. Faded prints are usually yellow in tone. Contrast can be increased by the use of an orthochromatic contrast film. Since the picture is yellowed, a filter of opposite color, such as blue, can also be of value in increasing contrast. But this will not eliminate any stains. In fact, it may emphasize them. So here again you are faced with a choice. Which is more important? The contrast or the stain? Well, it will be easier for the artist to work out the stain than it will be to build up the contrast with artwork and retouching.

JUDGING THE COPY NEGATIVE

After you have made your copy negative, what must you look for? How do you judge it?

First, we must check sharpness. Is the negative as sharp as it could be? Compare it with the original. As stated previously, with a sharp and clearly defined original, making the comparison is a simple matter. But when the picture image is soft, out of focus, or diffused, it is much more difficult to judge. We cannot expect the copy to be sharper than the original but we want to be sure that it is equally as sharp and no more diffused than the original.

Secondly, we must examine the contrast range of the negative. There should be strongly defined blacks and whites. The negative should not be overcontrasty. The grays must also be there. It will do you little good if you have obtained strong blacks and whites while losing the middle tones. You should try to avoid making a flat negative. Of course, this depends on the contrast range of the original itself. A strong, snappy print is going to make a better copy than a flat, faded one. This is true even though you have made use of contrast films, filters, etc., to build up the copy contrast. If the original is too contrasty, you have to avoid adding to it. Otherwise the negative will have only very strong blacks accompanied by washed out white areas and no middle tones. With such originals, a normal portrait film and developer will provide a better copy negative, for restoration purposes, than the contrasty copy film.

The third thing to check is details. A photograph is made up of varying shades from black through gray to white. These can be fine lines, broader lines, or large areas and form the details of the picture. If the copy is sharp and properly contrasted, there should be no appreciable loss of detail. But often in copying there will be a difference in contrast that will erase some details. Filtering can have the same effect. If the copy is not critically sharp, fine details will blur out. If you note that such details are missing, you should determine whether or not this is due to a change in contrast value or a loss of sharpness. If contrast is at fault, you must decide whether the change or improvement in contrast is more important than the lost details. This becomes a choice beween the lesser of two evils. Was a filter at fault? Here, too, you have a similar choice to make. Is it due to a lack of sharpness? Here, there is no choice. You should remake the negative, obtaining a sharper one.

Checking the copy negative is important. You must try to obtain the best possible results in copying. The quality of your workprint depends on the quality of the copy negative. A poor negative can only produce a poor print, which will mean additional retouching and restoration work and, in all probability, a finished job that is not as good as it could be.

Making copy negatives is not a mysterious or complicated process. It is simple to master. This chapter has only touched on the subject as it relates to the copy restoration work. If you want to investigate the subject further and go into other aspects of copying, there are more detailed manuals on the subject.

PROCEDURES FOR COPYING DIFFERENT TYPES OF ORIGINALS

Each type of original, as described in the last chapter, requires a different type of handling in copying. It is worthwhile to examine the procedure with each of these.

The Daguerreotype

Mounting to the copyboard. If you have removed the daguerreotype from the case for pre-copy treatment, it should be copied before being replaced in its case. The daguerreotype can be held to the copyboard by pushpins at the edges. The point of the pin cannot pierce the metal base of the picture, but the lips of the head can hold it fast to the board. Although thumbtacks can do the same job, pushpins are easier to

44. A normal and faded snapshot copied on the same type of film to show the difference in contrast obtained.

handle. If the daguerreotype is still in the case and is not to be removed for any reason, it can be held to the copyboard by using screw eyes, as described earlier.

Lighting. As has been noted before, the daguerreotype is reflective in nature. Many of them are almost perfect mirrors, with an image visible only when viewed at a proper angle. However, two lights at 45° angles bring the image out without reflection. It may be necessary to adjust and

45. Improved result obtained by copying faded original on a contrast process film.

readjust the position of the lights to get the image. Your point of viewing must be from behind the camera. You might not see an image that will be recorded by the camera if you look at the daguerreotype from either side of the board. This is where the ground glass view screen of the camera is important. If you can see the image there, you will get it on your copy. If you have to adjust the lights, it will tell you when you have got them in the correct spots. It is also very helpful to cover the front of the camera, the lens board, with something black, so that there will be no reflection from that point.

Film. Since these originals are monochromes, orthochromatic films should be used. Increase in contrast is usually necessary. The film should be of a contrast, commercial, or commercial process type and developed in a high contrast developer.

Filters. It is not usually necessary to use filters. The only stains we have noted on these originals are bluish in tone and occur at the edges of the print. A blue filter could help. But this requires the use of a panchromatic film and, as the daguerreotype itself often has a bluish cast, the filter might only serve to give you a softer copy negative. As contrast is more important, therefore, pass up the use of the filter.

The Ambrotype

Mounting to the copyboard. As with the daguerreotype, the ambrotype may or may not be in the case. If in the case, it can be held to the board with screw eyes; if not in the case, you must remember that you are dealing with a piece of glass. If you use pushpins or thumbtacks, do not press them in with too much force or you will crack the glass. It will be better to attach the glass ambrotype to a sheet of cardboard, using masking or adhesive tape along the edges to hold it to the cardboard, then attaching the card to the board with pushpins or tacks.

Lighting. Since we are dealing with glass, reflections must be avoided. While this reflection will not be as severe as those of some daguerreotypes, we can avoid them by using the same steps as we did with the daguerreotype. The use of a black-covered lens board is advisable.

Film. Use the same films as with the daguerreotype, since additional contrast is almost always required.

Filters. No filters are necessary.

The Tintype

Mounting to the copyboard. The tintype can be fastened directly on the copyboard with pushpins. It can also be taped first to a cardboard.

This may be more advantageous, for you can use the resulting sharp line as an aid in focusing.

Lighting. As the tintype is usually very dark, it should be lighted at 45° angles so that the most light possible falls on the picture. This dark aspect makes it difficult to see the image in the view screen and to focus it. Therefore, we suggest the use of the tape guide.

Film. It is of utmost importance to get the greatest degree of contrast possible. For this you should use a commercial process film with a very contrasty developer.

Filters. Since our objective is to build contrast, these cannot help.

Faded Prints

Mounting to the copyboard. These can be attached directly to the copyboard with pushpins or screw eyes, depending upon the base of the print. If it is curled or cracked, it should be placed in a printing frame, which can be held to the copyboard by the aid of large screw eyes, as was described earlier.

Lighting. Regular, even copy lighting is suggested.

Film. It is necessary to build up contrast, so a contrast film, such as commercial process films should be used, with a high-contrast type developer.

Filters. If the faded print has a yellowish tone, a blue filter should be used.

Grained Prints

Mounting to copyboard. Follow the same procedure used with faded prints.

Lighting. Lighting is important and very critical with this type of original. The light has to be adjusted so there is as little shadow effect as possible. This effect brings out the grain, which we do not want. If pre-copy treatment has been tried and was successful, then normal 45° lighting will be fine. But if not, then the angle used here will often cause shadows to fall in the valleys of the grain and produce a strong grain effect on the copy negative. This effect can be seen by close inspection of the view screen image.

When this occurs, we must seek another lighting arrangement. One alternative is to have the light reflectors face the copyboard directly instead of at 45° angles. The reflectors must be equidistant from the center line of the work being copied. They also must be far enough away from the copyboard so that the overlapping light from the two sources covers the entire picture and provides even lighting. Thus, it will be necessary to move the lights farther back when copying a large original than when copying a smaller one, so that the original falls within the overlapping cone of light. Grain and texture are less likely to be picked up here.

Another suggested arrangement involves the use of reflected light. Place white cards in the position usually occupied by the copy lights. Then place the copy lights in such a position that they shine on the cards instead of the copyboard, and the reflected light falls evenly on the picture being copied. The light that does fall on the copyboard will be less intense than the direct light, and an increased exposure will be necessary.

Polarized screens also can be used to cut down on reflections that cause the texture effect to be registered on the copy. Such screens are placed over the lens of the camera and over each light. When the axis or plane of the polarization of the screens that cover the lights is perpendicular to that of the one placed over the lens, most reflections from the texture grain should be eliminated. The axis of the screen covering the lens can be rotated so that the effect of the reflections coming through can be changed. Examination of the image on the view screen will enable

46. Two originals copied on the same sheet of film to show their relative size.

you to find the degree of rotation that will provide a copy negative with a minimum of texture reflection.

Film. The choice of film depends on the color, stains, etc., of the original.

Filters. The use of filters will also depend upon the condition of the print. We have already mentioned the use of polarized screens. The desirability of the purchase and use of such equipment will depend upon the number of grained originals you are required to finish and whether or not you have been able to reduce or eliminate such grain by the other methods that have been described to you.

Large Originals

Mounting to the copyboard. Screw eyes will usually be necessary, as pushpins may be too small to hold the picture to the board. But, if the print is doubleweight, pushpins can be used. However, if the print is curled, it should be mounted to a heavier cardboard and flattened (pre-copy work). This heavier mount will require screw eyes. If the large original is one of the oval convexed shapes, pushpins should be used at

47. The same two originals as in illustration #46, sized by copying so that each head is equalized for regrouping purposes.

the edges. These may have to pierce the edge. Often it will be sufficient to use one at the top and another at the bottom of the print.

Lighting. To insure even lighting, the copy lights must be moved farther away from the copyboard, so that the cone of overlapping light becomes larger. Otherwise you may get hot spots. The convex original may show glare at the edges, because of its shape. This can be reduced by adjusting the lights and examining the view screen, or by using reflectors and indirect lighting or polarized screens.

Film. The type of film depends on the original.

Filters. These, too, depend upon the nature of the original.

CHAPTER 4

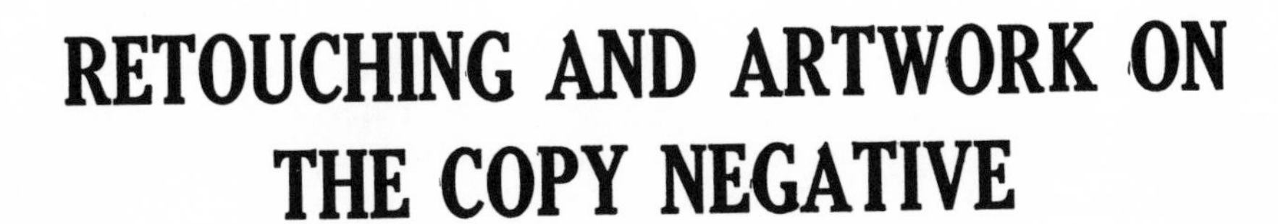

RETOUCHING AND ARTWORK ON THE COPY NEGATIVE

In each step of the restoration process we want to do as much as possible to complete the job. But, it is not always possible or expedient to do this. Therefore, we do as much as we can and leave the rest for the following steps.

So far we have tried to improve the original before copying by eliminating dirt, stains, grain and minimizing cracks, tears, folds, etc. What we could not do in this pre-copy treatment, we tried to do while copying. Now after copying many faults still remain. Some of these can be taken care of, to some extent at least, on the copy negative. A good deal of retouching and artwork can be accomplished here.

There will always be the question, at this step, whether it is of greater advantage to do such work on the copy negative or to save it for the workprint. There is no pat answer. This is something that the individual photo-restorer has to decide for himself. It will be a decision based upon experience, personal likes, aptitudes, and skills. Should the restorer find positive retouching easier than negative work, he will favor doing the work on the print rather than on the negative. The reverse is also true. You will understand this better after we discuss what can be done with the copy negative.

RETOUCHING TOOLS

Let's examine the tools with which we can work. We can retouch the copy negative with the aid of four basic tools: the retouching pencil, the spotting brush, the etching knife, and the air brush.

The Pencil

The lead pencil is one of the most popular tools used for retouching. The lead is applied locally to areas of the negative where the density should be increased so that part will print lighter. Any black spots or dark stains on the original will become light or thin areas on the negative. Applying lead to increase density here will eliminate or remove such spots.

These pencils are available in varying degrees of hardness, from a very hard lead to a very soft one. If you draw a soft lead across a sheet of white paper and then a hard lead, you will see that with the same pressure the soft one leaves a much darker line. The same effect takes place on the negative. The soft lead will make a darker mark and is useful in intensifying or filling in very weak or thin areas. The hard lead is utilized only where a slight correction in density is required.

The Spotting Brush

A fine spotting brush used with black water color does the same work as the pencil. If you mix the color as a thick solution, it will leave a dense black spot when applied to the negative. If you wish to make a finer correction, the solution can be thinned with water. However, the spotting brush is more difficult to use than the retouching pencil and is more bothersome. For instance, mixing the paint to a proper consistency is more time-consuming than choosing the desired grade of lead. There is work, such as blocking out the background, cutting around the figure, or blanking out a detail area, that only a brush can do. Spotting brushes are available in various widths to accommodate such jobs.

48. Basic retouching setup.

The Etching Knife

The etching knife is used to reduce the density of a specific area on the negative, so that more light will pass through at this point and print darker. This is accomplished by scraping away the emulsion at this point. For a total black effect, all the emulsion is scraped away until only the bare, clear celluloid backing is left. For intermediate shades of gray, less emulsion would be scraped away according to the effect desired. Doing this requires practice and skill, but it can be done. For an etching knife, you can use a special diamond-shaped scratch pen that fits into a standard pen holder. There are also specially made etching knives. Hobbyists' modeling knives can be used. Many retouchers use the edge of a broken razor blade. All of these do the same job and do it equally well. It is just a matter of which one the retoucher finds easiest to use.

The Air Brush

The air brush can be used to apply opaque paint to the negative. This will increase the density of a specific area, resulting in a white spot on the workprint. But there is a drawback here. Upon extreme enlargement, the air brush grain will show as white dots on the print. The air-brush color is sprayed on to the surface of the negative in the form of fine grains. If for any reason these are not fine enough, we get the white spots. This is one reason we want the copy negative to be as large as conveniently possible. If we have to treat it with the air brush, the less the amount of enlargement required to make the workprint, the less the degree of the grain that will show.

CORRECTION WORK

Theoretically, it is possible to do a complete restoration job on the copy negative by pure negative retouching, using the tools we have mentioned. However, this is not practical. It will take much more time than the positive retouching method, it is not as flexible, and it will not yield optimum results. So only those corrections that are the most practical as far as eliminating or minimizing work in later stages are the ones we are going to discuss.

Corrections by Spotting and Etching

Any flaw on the original will show up on the copy as a spot, series of spots, or lines. These will be either black or white and can be removed by etching or spotting. The black spots, which become light or thin spots on the negative, can be filled in and made denser with the proper lead pencil or spotting brush to blend in with the surrounding area. Conversely, the white spots, which show up as black or dense spots on the negative, can be reduced by careful use of the etching knife to blend in with the surrounding area.

Corrections by Blocking Out

Blocking is the application of opaque paint to a certain portion of the negative to prevent it from printing. The area becomes pure white on the workprint. This should be used only when we want to eliminate something entirely. If we want to get rid of a background, we can paint around the figure. If, for example, we want to change a bow tie to a long one, the vee area of the shirt can be blocked. Thus the bow is eliminated and a clean white area is left where the artist can draw in the new tie on the workprint. By the same reasoning, if a subject is wearing a checked shirt and a white one is desired, the checked shirt can be blocked and the details of a white shirt put on the now clean area. The blocked area has to be rebuilt on the workprint. Blocking saves much labor when working on the print, because, if the area had not been blocked, the artist would have to whiten it by applying opaque air-brush color or by bleaching it with cyanide. Both of these methods are more time-consuming than blocking.

The air brush can be used for blocking. By staying away from the outline of the figure, a softer effect can be obtained. A stencil or mask can be used to protect the figure if you want to get close to it. If any of the air-brush color should get on the figure, it can be washed off with water, using a small piece of absorbent cotton.

The objection to blocking, however, is the hard outline and cutout effect that results. This has to be softened down and blended by positive retouching.

A BASIC ARRANGEMENT FOR RETOUCHING NEGATIVES

To do this work properly, you need some sort of working arrangement. You must have a steady stand to hold the work. It must be translucent so that a light can be placed behind it to illuminate the negative and let you see what you are doing. And it must be kept on a table or stand so that you can sit down or do your work comfortably.

A sheet of ground glass or white-opal milk glass should be placed

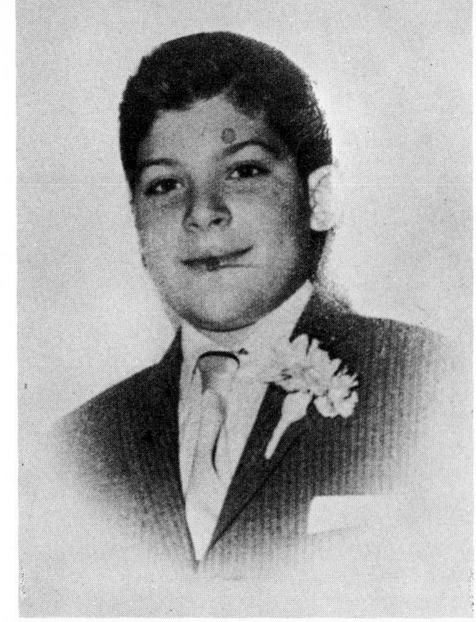

49. (LEFT) *Result obtained by blocking subject's head from group negative (see illustration #29) by use of a handbrush and black paint. Note hard outline.*

50. (RIGHT) *Softer result obtained by blocking head by means of airbrush and stencil.*

51. (LEFT) *An original with dark spots on the face and white lace area.*

52. (RIGHT) *Improvement obtained by spotting negative with retouching pencil or spotting brush.*

into a steady wooden frame. Clear glass will not do, as it cannot diffuse the light. The sheet of glass should be large enough to accommodate any size negative; it should be no smaller than 8″ x 10″. When working on a small negative, the glass should be covered by a card with an opening in it large enough to accommodate only the negative on which you are working. This allows you to concentrate on the work you have to do and keeps your eye from being distracted by a large sheet of illuminated glass. It also prevents eye fatigue.

This frame should be placed at a 45° angle for the most comfortable working. It can be supported by some sort of an arm, brace, or angle iron to keep it steady at this position. This can be placed against a window, and daylight can be used for a light source. However, this limits you to daytime hours and makes you dependent upon weather conditions. Artificial illumination is more practical. This can be supplied by an ordinary light bulb. The strength of the bulb depends on the individual. Still, the bulb must not be too weak for the light to show up the negative, nor must it be so strong that it will hurt your eyes. A denser negative will require a stronger light behind it than a thinner negative.

Your tools should be kept in a handy place, so that you can get at them easily and not lose time looking for what you need. You can vary your arrangement for retouching negatives according to your needs or to the materials you have at your disposal. Retouching stands can be obtained at any photographic stock house, if you want to invest the money. Or you can build one yourself at a minimal expense. It is up to you.

REVIEWING CORRECTION WORK ON COPY NEGATIVES

At the risk of repetition, we are going to identify special faults and describe the methods of correcting them. We are classifying these as work on the background, the clothing, and the face, and we will refer to these divisions more and more as we get into the retouching and artwork. There may be some confusion about the terms "black spots" and "white spots," since we discuss negatives in one chapter and positive prints in another. To maintain a standard term reference and to avoid any confusion, these terms will refer to the spots as they appear on the original and on the workprint; in other words, as positive images. The black spot on the original will show up as a clear or transparent spot on

53. (LEFT) *Improvement obtained by retouching crack, see illustration #25, on copy negative with an etching knife.*

54. (CENTER) *Portion of copy negative to show crack treated by airbrush.*

55. (RIGHT) *Result of treating crack by airbrush as it will appear on the workprint.*

the negative, but it will still be referred to as the "black spot." The white spot will show up black on the negative but will still be referred to as the "white spot."

Corrections on the Background

Black spots. They should be removed by spotting with a medium or soft lead pencil. A fine spotting brush, dipped in black water or spotting color, can also be used. The spots should be filled in or darkened to increase the density and match or blend in with the surrounding area.

White spots. They have to be reduced in density so that light can pass through and register on the print. Small spots can be handled with a fine-pointed etching knife. The objective is to scrape away the emulsion here, thus reducing the local density. On wider areas or large spots, the use of the fine-pointed blade can consume too much time. An etching knife with a broader, chisel-like edge should be used.

Cracks. Upon examination, the crack appears as a series of black-and-white lines and as black-and-white irregular spots. You have to try to fill

56. Improvement obtained by treating hole in print by retouching with etching knife on copy negative (see illustration #27). Note how cropping has eliminated torn bottom area.

in the black spots and etch out the white ones, blending them into the adjoining picture area in order to remove or minimize the crack. This will require much time and work, and, in the majority of cases, the retouching will show on the workprint and require further work to cover it. Another method of treating the crack is to go over it very carefully with air-brush opaque. This will leave a soft white line on the workprint, which can be filled in by positive retouching, artwork, and airbrushing. When a crack runs through an area of the picture that has no detail, such as a plain background, this method will be less time consuming and yield smoother results than retouching and etching.

Blocking. This is accomplished by the use of a wider spotting or water-color brush and an opaque, water-based paint. This can be black, red, or opaque gray. The important thing for the paint to do is hold back the light. The paint is applied to the background area and lined

57. Copy negative, see illustration #20, which has been retouched by airbrush to whiten background and cover black marks and cracks on face.

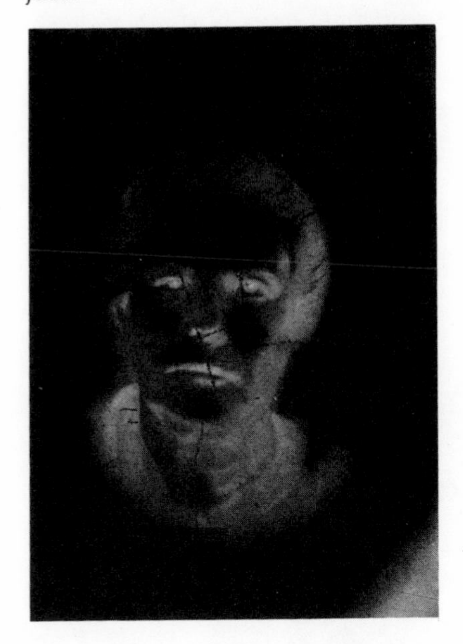

58. Workprint obtained from airbrush copy negative. Note how facial areas that have been airbrushed become bleached out.

around the edges of the figure. The result on the workprint will be a pure white background with a cutout figure appearing on it.

Air-brush blocking. The same effect can be obtained with the air brush. Here the figure must be protected by a cutout frisket, or mask, that covers the figure and prevents the air-brush color from falling on it. When this frisket is removed, the result is a blocked background with a clean figure on it.

Air-brush blocking without the frisket. This method involves a more skillful use of the air brush since we are dispensing with the use of a frisket. The air-brush color is sprayed on to the areas of the background away from the figure. The figure can be protected by a hand stencil, held in the left hand and moved to protect the figure in coordination with the movement of the air brush in the right hand. This produces a vignetted effect, with the background close to the figure and blending out to white as it goes away from the figure. This does away with the cutout effect and allows the artist to work in a blended background on the workprint

59. Copy negative (see illustration #43), with heads regrouped by cutting negative, raising lady's head, and taping separate parts of trimmed negative in proper position.

without the use of opaque. Should any air-brush color get on the figure, it can be washed off with cotton and water.

Using the air brush to blot out special areas of the background. In the case where just part of a background is damaged and you want to retain the general effect, you can use the air brush to cover or blank out the damaged area. This will produce a white area on the workprint that can be filled in by air brush to match the rest of the background.

Corrections on Clothing

Spots and cracks. Since there is actually no difference between a spot or a crack that appears on the clothing area and a spot or a crack that appears on the background, the treatment is the same, and further details are not necessary.

Altering or changing clothing. When you only want to alter some part of the subject's clothes, local blocking by hand brush or air brush will cover the undesired item and leave a white area on the workprint where the artist can rebuild a new article of clothing. For example, should you want to replace a dark shirt or a tee shirt with a collar and

60. Resultant workprint from regrouped copy negative.

tie, painting a vee beneath the neckline will provide a suitable white area for that work.

When you want to change the clothing entirely, such as replacing informal clothes with a suit and tie, or a shirtwaist with a dress, you can cover the entire clothing area within the outlines by hand-brush blocking or by air-brush opaquing to obtain a white area on the workprint where you can draw in and build up the new clothing.

Correcting shoulder lines, necklines, or lapel lines. Corrections of this kind can be made by pencil or knife. If the shoulder is darker than the background and is too high, it can be lowered by using the pencil to make the area denser and bring down the tone of the background to the desired changed line. If the background is darker than the shoulder, an etching knife can be used to reduce the density at the shoulder line and bring down the darker background to the desired line. Very often a jowl runs over the subject's collar. The collar line can be raised by penciling in the part of the jowl that covers the white collar. A spotting brush

61. Regrouping and joining of two separate copy negatives (see illustration #46). Note overlapping of bodies. Also note how printed ribbons across woman's chest have been blocked out by handbrush opaquing on the negative. Note airbrush work on background.

can also be used here. Crooked lapels can be straightened by using the pencil to blend in the crooked parts of the line while the etching knife can be used to join or bring together the straight portions.

Facial Corrections

Work done on the face and features of the subject must be handled with more care than the work done on backgrounds or clothing. Especially with work on a negative, a mistake in retouching can change the character or destroy the "likeness" of the subject. No matter how proficiently any other work is done, if the character is changed, the restoration is not a successful one.

Cracks and spots. They should be treated with pencil and knife only. This is true even if the crack is a large one and could be handled, seemingly, with air-brush opaque. Using the air brush is not a good idea because a certain percentage of the spray will go over on to the rest of the face and can blur or fog a vital feature. When a crack or a spot covers

62. Workprint obtained from copy negative (see illustration #61).

part of the mouth, eyes, or nose, retouching must be done very carefully so as not to cause any change of appearance.

Heavy lines and wrinkles. They can be softened, reduced, or removed with the lead pencil or the etching knife. Here, too, care must be exercised, for in making corrections of these natural facial faults, likeness can be lost or character changed. It may seem that the use of the air brush, with transparent color instead of opaque, would be ideal to increase some density and thus soften such lines and wrinkles without completely removing them. However, this process is a difficult one to control; the danger of white dots from air-brush grain exists and some airbrushing may go over the rest of the face. This is not, however, to rule out such use. But the drawbacks must be pointed out. When you use it, and how well, depends on you.

As we proceed to the next stages in the restoration process, you will see that most of the work which can be done, as we have described, on the primary copy negative can also be done on the workprint by positive retouching and airbrushing. Which will be used is a matter of individual choice; it is up to the photo-restorer. The use of negative work will cut down on the work and time necessary to finish the workprint. Photo-restoration is a combination of photography, retouching, and artwork. Some faults can be eliminated by photographic correction, negative retouching, positive retouching, or artwork (*i.e.,* each of these can be used to correct the fault). If one is resorted to, the others need not be utilized. Some photo-restorers are stronger in photography, some are more skilled in retouching, and some are most apt as artists. They will tend to lean most heavily on the strongest skill: the photographer will try to do most of his correction work while copying and making the workprint; the retoucher, by work on the negative; the artist, by artwork on the workprint.

As you gain experience, you also will tend to rely on your strongest skill. You will also find that there are some faults it is best to correct with one method, and others with another. There are times when it is best to remove a spot on the copy negative; other times when it is better to leave it for the workprint.

This book can only tell you so much. Experience will have to provide the rest.

CHAPTER 5

MAKING THE WORKPRINT

We are assuming that the reader understands the process of making enlarged prints from photographic negatives and is able to do so. Therefore, we will not go into the subject of how to make prints, but we will discuss making enlarged prints for photo-restoration—that is, specifically as photo-restoration workprints.

PURPOSE OF THE WORKPRINT

What should you expect from the workprint? What should it contribute towards the completed restoration job? If you have been able, up to this point, to do a fairly complete restoration job by (1) cleaning the original in the pre-copy stage, (2) making corrections and overcoming faults while copying, and (3) working on the copy negative, you can expect the workprint to become the final finished print requiring, at most, a little positive retouching. This will hold true for what may be called "easy" jobs, those in which the original is not too badly damaged and which call for no changes or corrections.

In the majority of restoration jobs, where much of the restoration work must be done on a positive print, the workprint must become the vessel for the air-brush work and positive retouching that will be necessary to complete the job properly. The workprint can be finished primarily for purposes of recopying or reproduction, or it can be finished so that it is a final print in itself and can be mounted, framed, or exhibited.

THE WORKPRINT INTENDED FOR RECOPYING

When the print is intended for recopying, it should have a smooth and ungrained surface. If no pencil work is going to be required, a glossy surface can be used. However, if you do use glossy paper, do not ferrotype it. The ferrotyping will reject the air-brush work, and to make the print workable, you will have to remove the ferrotyping by rubbing with pumice stone or rewashing. If you are going to have to do pencil retouching or pastel work, a matte paper will better accept the work. No grain is wanted because a smooth surface will give you a better recopy and you will not have to work to overcome the grain. If much air-brush opaque color will have to be used on a particular restoration job, the workprint should be recopied. When opaque air-brush work is used, especially on black-and-white prints, the work takes a bluish cast or tone which is unnatural and to which many people object. This is lost when the print is recopied, and the recopy print takes on natural print tones. Also, there is the possibility of very heavy airbrushing cracking or peeling after a period of time. While this does not often happen, if it does, and the workprint has been recopied, it does not matter.

THE WORKPRINT AS A FINAL PRINT

If your positive retouching will require the air brush to use only transparent colors or a very minimal amount of opaque work, the completed workprint can be used as a final print. The transparent air-brush colors lend themselves to the natural tone of the print. Black, when diluted, is transparent and does not create an artificial cast. Because recopying is not of prime consideration, you are free to use any portrait paper, grained or not, that will provide you with the most attractive print surface for the restored portrait. Portrait paper is available in various grades and surfaces; any can be used. This will be discussed later in the chapter on recopying.

SPECIAL TECHNIQUES

To obtain a good workprint, you must do more than make a straight enlargement from the copy negative. It is important that you make the print in such a manner that it leaves the least amount of work possible for the positive retoucher. You should take advantage, therefore, of all

63. (LEFT) *Copy print of an old photo in its original format.*

64. (RIGHT) *Head and shoulder area of same original enlarged and cropped.*

the techniques or "tricks" available to you to achieve this result. These include cropping, vignetting, burning in, and dodging.

Cropping

Cropping involves cutting out unwanted portions of the original picture from the workprint by making the enlargement bigger than the sheet of photographic paper and allowing only the desired picture area to be printed. This method is often used when the edges of an original are badly damaged and not important enough to merit restoring. Cropping is used when you wish to take out a subject from a group and when you wish to make a head and shoulders portrait from a full figure original.

Vignetting

Suppose you crop out the head of a subject and find that, in eliminating unwanted details at the edges of the print, you have to print the head too large and you obtain a composition that is crowded. One way to overcome this is to print a smaller head, in proper proportions, and keep out the objectionable edges by vignetting.

Vignetting is accomplished by preventing light from falling on certain portions of the printing paper. These portions are white on the final print. The parts held back are usually those at the outer edges of the print so that only the subject in the center is visible, with the surrounding background fading off into white.

A similar effect can be obtained by airbrushing the copy negative. Which method is the better? It depends upon the job. Each restoration job is an individual one with problems of its own. No one job is exactly like another. Thus you will find occasions when airbrushing the copy negative can be more helpful than vignetting the print.

However, in the main, vignetting proves to be more efficient than airbrushing the negative. Vignetting is accomplished while making the workprint. It saves you the step of having to work upon the negative in the previous stage and thus it eliminates the work and time necessary to do that air-brush work. Also, while there is the possibility of air-brush grain with the latter method, this does not exist with vignetting.

Thus, with simple vignettes, this is a more efficient method. What about vignetting more complicated figures or outlines? In such cases,

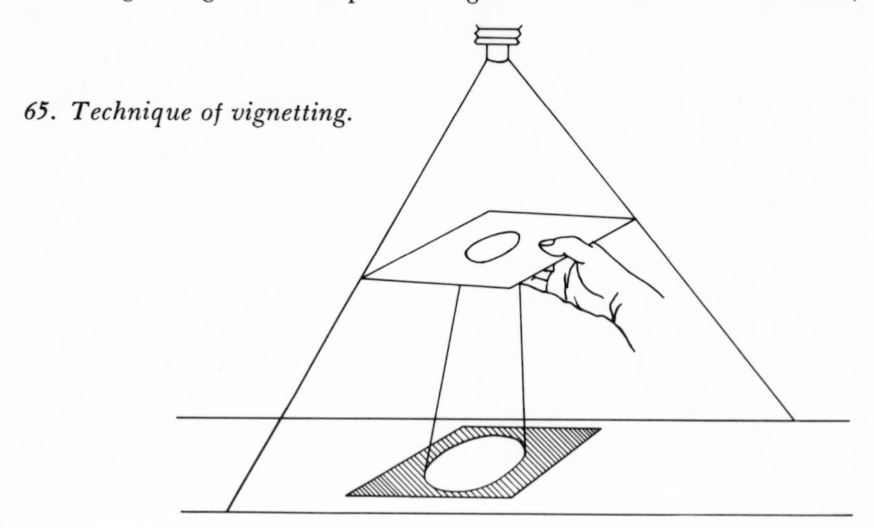

65. Technique of vignetting.

you can get around the figure better with the air brush. But you must contend with the grain and, of course, control the air brush. Can you vignette? Yes, if you can cut out a special mask to fit the outlines of the figure in question. This can be done by placing a cardboard or sheet of thick, opaque paper so that the image from the enlarger falls upon it. You then trace the outline with a soft pencil and cut it out with a scissors. This then becomes the mask you hold between the printing paper and lens, thus withholding light from all portions of the printing paper except the main image. Cutting out a special mask should involve no more, if not less, time than airbrushing the copy negative. All things considered, vignetting should give you a better workprint.

To vignette, a card is held between the lens of the enlarger and the printing paper. The basic idea behind this technique, as well as that of dodging and burning in, is the blocking of light from a specified or particular area of the print. The same thing is accomplished by airbrushing the negative; that is, we hold back light from paper so that it is not exposed. The length of time that this card is held there, in relation to the total exposure time, determines how much of the image is kept from being registered.

66. (LEFT) *Cropped portion of snapshot (see illustration #44).*

67. (RIGHT) *Effect obtained by vignetting same print.*

68. (LEFT) *Effect obtained by vignetting to eliminate hard oval (see illustration #15).*

69. (RIGHT) *Vignetted workprint from copy negative, see illustration #64, which has been airbrushed to eliminate portions of the head of lady on the left.*

The vignetting mask has a hole cut or torn out of its center to permit the passage of light. The opening can be round, oval, square, or cut out to fit around the figure in question, as we have described before. If you hold this card still for the entire length of the exposure, you will obtain a rather hard outline. Since the card is held some distance away from the paper, the outline will not be sharp, but it will be diffused to some extent. If, however, you move the card up and down rhythmically or jiggle it from side to side, the edges will be softer, since the intermittent holding back of light from the edges of the mask will cause the background to blend into the white. It is important to get the knack of keeping the vignetter in motion. The softer you can get the edge, the smoother the effect of blending and, consequently, the easier it will be to finish the workprint.

Burning in

The effect of vignetting can be reversed so as to have the background fade into black instead of white. This is often called "burning in" or dark vignetting. To get this effect, a reverse form of the vignetter is used. A round, oval, or other-shaped cutout card is held over the figure to keep the light from it while overexposing the edges. This is done only after a normal exposure is made, to obtain the proper print quality as far as the important figure is concerned. A thin wire or glass stirring rod should be attached to the card as a handle. If you hold the card in place with your hand, the shadow of your hand will hold back some part of the burned-in area. With a wire or glass rod the line of attachment will not be noticeable, especially if you move it about during the exposure. Moving the card, as prescribed for vignetting, is necessary to soften the edges of the "burn in."

The final effect of "burning in" will give you a print with black edges and a dark vignette or halo effect. This is an effective way of drawing attention to the subject in the center of the picture and of de-emphasizing distracting objects along the edges.

Dodging

Dodging is a technique of holding back a certain amount of light from a specified local area of the overall print so that it will print lighter than it would on the straight enlargement. This is a form of local control. Any area that is too dark on the straight print can be lightened by dodging. Conversely, any area that prints too light can be strengthened by holding back, or dodging, all other areas of the print except the one that needs the extra exposure.

Dodging is accomplished in much the same manner as "burning in." A similar tool is used. It may be smaller in size than that used for the "burning," since the area you want to hold back may be a small or very local one. A reverse type tool, for example, a card that covers the entire picture except for a small hole in the center, should be used to apply extra exposure to an area that requires stronger printing than the rest of the picture.

When making prints from copy negatives of old, stained, and damaged photos, you will find many instances where the use of these techniques will enable you to produce a cleaner print, to subdue or even eliminate some glaring faults, and to reduce the amount of positive retouching work required in the finishing step.

CRITERIA FOR JUDGING YOUR WORKPRINT

Standards for judging the workprint differ somewhat from those you would use for a regular portrait, commercial, studio, or exhibition print.

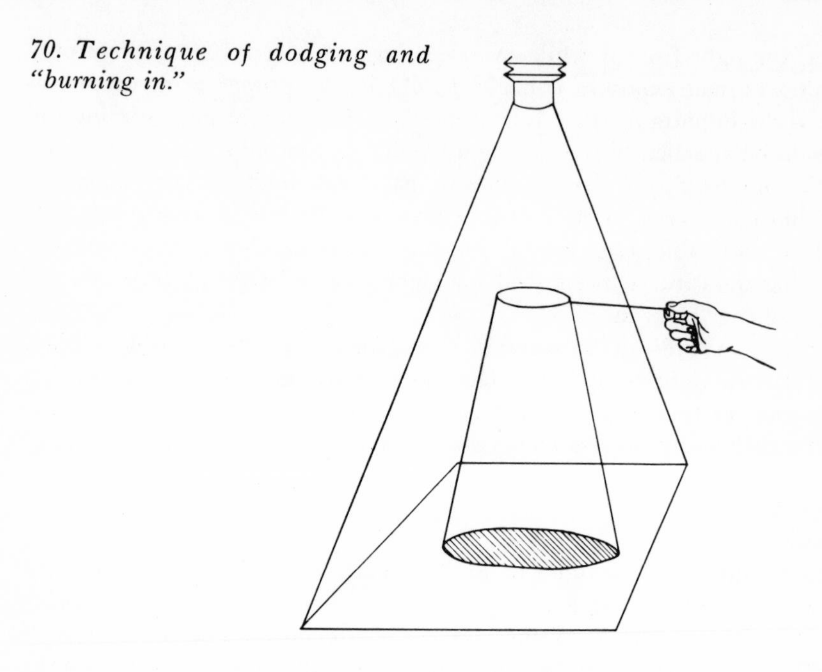

70. Technique of dodging and "burning in."

This is, of course, because of the special purpose for which the workprint has been made (*i.e.,* to provide the best possible vessel for the positive retouching and restoration artwork).

Sharpness

The first thing to look for is sharpness. The workprint must be as critically sharp as it can possibly be. While it is permissible or desirable to diffuse portrait and pictorial prints to obtain a soft effect, to subdue retouching, or to eliminate the need for retouching, this is not true for the workprint. There is no room for diffusion or loss of whatever sharpness or clarity the original possesses. This is especially true when we deal with group originals that have fine feature details. It only takes a slight amount of diffusion, whether in copying or printing, to lose the character of the eyes, nostrils, or lips. And these are very important!

When the original is sharp, it is simple to judge whether or not the copy print is equally as sharp. That is all we can expect; we can not expect it to be any sharper. This statement may seem unnecessary, but we have to deal with many originals that are not really sharp. They may have been diffused deliberately or they may be out of focus. The latter is very often the case with snapshot originals. So, when the original is not sharp, the copy print cannot be sharp. This is obvious. But we do not want the workprint to be any less sharp than the original. This is not as easy to judge as it would be if the original were sharp. Extra pains have to be taken in examining the negative, comparing it to the original, and checking the copy negative.

It is with these out-of-focus originals that you can run into trouble when retouching and restoring the workprint, as far as likeness or character is concerned. This will be discussed in the next chapter. The point is that the chance of such difficulty is greater if the workprint is not as sharp as it could be.

If we find the print could be sharper, we should check to see whether the fault lies in the copy negative or whether it was due to the printing. If the work has to be redone, it is better to do it now than to proceed with the job and lose a further investment in labor, because, in all probability, the job will not be successful.

Strength

Having checked sharpness, the next thing we must look for is "strength." We want a workprint that retains or clearly brings out all the details and tones that are present in the original picture. In copying normal, undamaged, or unfaded photographs, some loss of detail is to be expected. This does not mean you must not try to get your copy as close to the original as possible. You should reproduce the halftones and medium grays and retain, as far as possible, the same tonal range.

Damaged, stained, or faded originals present another problem. They can be improved by copying and producing a workprint that is better than the original, even though it still requires artwork and retouching. This is especially true of faded originals where an increase in contrast can bring out details the eye cannot see.

It is possible to make your workprint too light. There is a tendency to keep such a print on the lighter side because it appears cleaner. Some of the dirt or stains will not show up as badly as on a stronger print. But, by keeping this print light, we lose important detail and tones. The lighter grays will fade into white and the print will be flat. To render a good restoration then, the retoucher will have to build up or replace the missing tones and details. This is extra work. If it can be avoided by proper printing, it should be. Artwork should be relied upon to do only what photography cannot!

Therefore, the workprint should be no lighter than a normal print made for other purposes. If bringing out the fold of a dress or the detail of some lace means also bringing out some dirt or marks, do so. It is wiser to remove the marks than to rebuild the fold or lace. In some instances it may seem easier to do the latter. But the final result will be more natural if we retouch the spots rather than rebuild missing details.

Here is where dodging technique is valuable. Often, in trying to bring out strength in a white dress, the facial area will become too dark. By dodging, you can hold back light from the area to obtain the proper facial tones while printing the dress stronger.

Now it may seem that a workprint is too dark or a little too much on the dark side, due to the requirement of bringing out as much detail as possible. However, you will find that the application of artwork and air-brush retouching will overcome this effect. Also, even if the finished workprint still appears to be on the strong side, a slightly more contrasty and lighter recopy print will take care of this.

When printing a negative that has been airbrushed, especially in a local area, you will have a tendency to print too dark. This actually does not occur in the exposure, but in the developing. So to be more accurate, we should say there would be a tendency to overdevelop the print. The reason for this is that the printer, while developing the print, notices the white spot (which had been airbrushed on the copy negative) and unconsciously tries to bring it up to match the rest of the print. Thus, while the spot remains white, the surrounding print area becomes too dark. This tendency, once recognized, can be overcome by experience.

Contrast

The third criterion is contrast. The use of various types of film, developers, and printing papers gives you a degree of control over the contrast of the workprint. Thus in copying and printing you can increase the contrast of a flat or faded original and decrease the contrast of an overly contrasty original. In considering contrast, we must take into account three types of original: the faded and flat one, the highly contrasted one, and the average one with a normal range of tones.

With the faded original, the more contrast you can gain, the better. You should have used contrast process films and developers in making the copy negative. You should use a contrast paper in getting the workprint.

The opposite is true of the original with very strong blacks, flat whites, and little or no middle tones. We should, of course, not do anything to increase this contrast. Therefore, use softer copy material and make a softer print. The result will be one in which the blacks become a dark gray and the whites go into a light gray. The appearance will be

71. Effect obtained by "burning in" the edges. Only a minimum of air-brush work will be necessary to finish this print.

like a fogged print. But it must be remembered that the print is going to be worked on by the restoration artist. He is going to pull out the highlights that have been fogged by soft printing; he is going to blacken the shadows that have become gray and add details or suggest details as necessary. He will convert the supposedly fogged print into one of a normal or more pleasing contrast range. He can best do this with a soft print.

With originals of normal or average contrast, there is something else to consider. What effect will any change in the contrast have upon the finished job? With such originals, a change in contrast can have an unsatisfactory effect. Let us consider a professional studio portrait as our original. Do not take into account any cracks, damages, or stains. Think only about the contrast range. On such an original we will find blacks in the clothing areas, if the clothing is dark. But details such as folds, creases, lapels, pockets, and buttons are also there. They may be one or two tones lighter than the over-all black of the clothing, but this difference is enough to reveal these details. If we add to the contrast of the copy, the whole area can go into black and the details will disappear. Sometimes this may be an improvement. If the clothing is poorly draped or wrinkled and unkempt, the darkening will hide these faults.

With white clothing, similar details are made up of light gray tones. An increase in contrast can bleach these into the white mass. Thus such details as lace, creases, folds, and seams disappear. Some of these, such as lace, can be very intricate in design, and if lost in copying, can present a time-consuming job. On the other hand, there is sometimes so much dirt and stains affecting this area that cleaning may present a more formidable retouching job. In this event, a bleached white area, eliminating such dirt, may be preferable; it may be easier to rebuild the details. This would seem to run counter to what we have said above. It does. This will illustrate the difficulty in making rules and the necessity for the photo-restorer to make certain decisions. Which is the lesser of two evils? To clean out the dirt by retouching, or to rebuild details with artwork? Part of the answer will depend upon your skill as an artist, part of it upon the intricacy of the detail work in question. A man's white shirt would be a simple job; a lady's white lace blouse would be an intricate one. The decision requires experience. As you become more familiar with photo-restoration work, you will learn which path you should take and which method is easier for you. It should be noted that what is easier for one photo-restorer may be more difficult for another.

The effect of contrasts on backgrounds is not of great importance and requires little discussion. The only time we must watch for contrast change, as far as the background is concerned, is when there is only a slight degree of variation in tone between the subject's hair and the background. This occurs often with a dark background and a subject with dark hair or with a subject with light blonde, white, or light gray hair against a white or light gray background. With a gain in contrast, background and hair can blend together with a loss of the hairline.

The most important part of any restoration job, as has been mentioned before, is the face. While restoring the photograph, or just a selected portion of it, we are also restoring the image of the subject of the photograph. If we do a good job of restoration but the subject of the restoration does not resemble the subject of the original, the job is a failure. Photographers speak of "likeness and character" when referring to the subject of a portrait. When a change in resemblance appears, this is called "losing the likeness."

There are many reasons why this happens in retouching, rebuilding a face, artwork, etc. These will be discussed in the following chapter. But we sometimes find that the likeness can be lost in the copying process, or in making the workprint. How is this possible?

Can a contrast change cause a change of likeness? It can in certain instances. A contrast increase can turn blonde or light brown hair, which should register as a medium or lighter gray tone, to a dark gray or black. It can darken eyes. It can lose certain details and highlights in hair or heavily shadowed areas of the face. Any one of these, alone or in combination, can cause the subject to appear different on the copy print than on the original photograph.

When we start with an original that is dull, gray, or flat, increasing contrast will give us a print that is snappier and appears clearer. This is desirable, and we want to get this improvement. But should it, for any reason, change the likeness or appearance of the subject from what is on the original, the improvement is of little or no value. This effect will not happen to many originals. It only occurs to a few, but it is something that has to be watched for and taken into account.

Thus once more you, as a photo-restorer, are faced with a decision. In this case, the choice of a flat workprint versus a more contrasty and snappier one, with reference to the retention of the character of the original subject. The ability to solve it can only come with experience. You must expect to learn by trial and error.

SIZE

One further consideration in making your workprint is the size. This may not seem too important at first, but we do have to determine the optimum size for a certain workprint. Three factors can affect workprint size. One is the size and the clarity of your original photo. The second is the desired size of the final prints. The third is the type of detail work that is required by the nature of the original.

Size and Clarity of the Original

When the original is small, diffused, or out of focus, do not expect it to become sharper and clearer upon enlargement. On the contrary, the diffusion will increase and become more apparent. Very often, because of its small size, an original appears to be sharp. But enlargement will prove this apparent sharpness is false. You will feel, when inspecting the workprint, that you have lost the sharpness in copying or enlarging. You should check back to be sure of your focusing. But you will find that, despite proper and sharp focus work, the enlargement is softer.

This means that the original is not as sharp as it appears. You can double check this effect by the use of a powerful magnifying glass.

For the sake of convenience the average size workprint is 8″ x 10″. This is a standard size. But if the original is very small or such that it cannot stand much enlargement, the 8″ x 10″ size may prove too large. It may be too soft or badly defined. It may reveal too much enlarged grain. In such a case, a 4″ x 5″ or a 5″ x 7″ workprint should be made.

But suppose, for some reason, it is necessary to bring such an original up to a large size, say 8″ x 10″, 11″ x 14″, or larger. Can anything be done to accomplish this? There is a way to do this. It is a step-up method. You start with a small workprint, for example, 4″ x 5″. This is built up and recopied. Then a larger workprint, say 8″ x 10″, is made. This will still require artwork to obtain a smooth effect and clean up the enlarged retouching and artwork from the smaller workprint. If a larger print is required, the process should be repeated. This may seem to entail extra work, especially in copying and making workprints. However, each step acts as a proof of the work. And the final result will yield a better likeness than if you stretched the copy to the desired size and retouched and built it up.

Desired Size of the Final Prints

Why should the size of the finished prints or recopy prints have any bearing on the size of the workprint, regardless of the size of the original? The answer lies in the fact that the finished workprint is a repository of pencil marks, etching marks, and air-brush grain. On a properly finished workprint these marks should blend into the picture and not be noticeable. (There are exceptions to this, where an extraordinary amount of retouching is required.) However, on an enlarged recopy print, the magnification will bring out the evidence of the hand and airbrush work. This means additional positive retouching on the recopy print which, if there are a number of duplicate prints involved, will mean a multiplication of the work. This extra work can be avoided.

It has been stated that the best overall or average size for your workprint is 8″ x 10″. It is not so small as to make detail work difficult and it is not so large as to be difficult to handle. When the final prints are to be 8″ x 10″ or smaller, this size workprint is fine. When the final prints are to be larger (up to 11″ x 14″), an 8″ x 10″ workprint, if very carefully finished, will do. Of course, an 11″ x 14″ workprint would be better. However, if you want your final prints to be 16″ x 20″, the 8″ x 10″

workprint may prove too small, the 11″ x 14″ would be better, and a 16″ x 20″ workprint would be best.

The larger workprints may prove unwieldy and will take more time to finish. The main reason for the use of these equal-size workprints is, as stated before, to avoid the enlargement and emphasis of retouching marks and air-brush grain. But it is possible for a very carefully worked 8″ x 10″ to yield only a minimum of faults on 11″ x 14″ or 16″ x 20″ final print. There are ways, when airbrushing, to obtain a very fine grain effect and to retouch without too much pencil work showing. You should always figure on doing a little more positive retouching on the final prints no matter what the size. There is always some spotting that must be done on any print. We will go into more details in the chapter devoted to recopy prints.

Effect of Details

The presence of fine details in the original can also influence the size of your workprint. It is much easier on your eyes, when you have an original such as a group photo, to work on a larger workprint. A smaller one will require the use of magnifying glasses and very close work. Such originals are usually sharp and can stand enlargement, so the larger workprint can be made. Then, again, a smaller detailed workprint will not produce a good recopy print of a larger size, as the work done to the details will become too obvious and perhaps objectionable. With originals such as these, the same size or reduced recopy prints are advisable, since the workprint size will also depend upon this.

To summarize, you must regard making the workprint as something different from making a regular print. The workprint has a specific purpose that the others do not; it provides a base for positive retouching and restoration work. It is with this in mind that the print should be made.

CHAPTER 6

POSITIVE RETOUCHING AND RESTORATION WORK ON THE WORKPRINT

Here is where you will make or break the restoration job. Up to now, everything you have done has been in preparation for this stage of the work. You have endeavored by pre-copy work, by copying techniques, by retouching the copy negative, and by special workprint printing to obtain a print that is as improved or restored as could be. But we did not expect these to be able to do the entire job. We hoped they would make the positive retouching step easier by eliminating much work.

This is the cleanup step. Whatever you could not fix before will be remedied now. If you have been unable to clean an original or treat the copy negative, this step will catch it. It may be a bit more difficult and time-consuming than other steps, but it will be done here. This is the step that requires the skill of the retoucher, the artist, and the air-brush operator. This is the step that requires the most patience and takes the longest time to master.

WHAT IS POSITIVE RETOUCHING?

What is positive retouching? It can be described as the process of repairing, fixing, spotting, and improving a print by working upon it with a retouching pencil, spotting brush, etching knife, chalk, pastel, water colors, or air brush.

The difference between positive and negative retouching is simply that with positive retouching the work is done on the positive print rather than on the negative film. Positive retouching is more easy and manageable than negative retouching. You can do more with it. You have more control. You are able to work upon a larger surface. Negative sizes are limited; 8″ x 10″ negatives are seldom used. Most are smaller than 5″ x 7″, which gives you a small area for working. Print sizes, on the other hand, are not so limited. You can get a print the size you want. Then again, retouching a negative means working with light coming through the transparency. This is harder on the eyes. Also, black and white values are reversed, which makes it harder to judge your progress than with a positive.

There are more tools and materials available to the positive retoucher to complete his work. He is not limited to the retouching pencil and etching knife. He can use charcoal and pastels, tortillon stumps, crayon sauces, colored pencils, transparent oils, and the air brush. Most of these are not adaptable to work on the negative.

Possibly the most important advantage is that you can see what you are doing and judge the effect of your work as it is being done.

POSITIVE RETOUCHING TOOLS

In discussing the tools we use for positive retouching, we may repeat what has been written previously about the tools used in negative work, since the negative tools are also of use in positive work. However, there are variations in application that must be mentioned.

Carbon and Lead Pencils

The pencil is the simplest retouching tool. Yet, despite its simplicity it can accomplish much work, and skill in its use is required. It is possible, although extremely time-consuming, to complete some positive retouching restorations using only the retouching pencil.

Retouching pencils for positive use come in different grades. There are two types: lead pencils and carbon pencils. Both come in varying grades from hard to soft. The carbons are softer than the leads and are used for heavier shading or working in dark shadow areas. In such an area, when you want to remove a white spot, the result must blend in with the surrounding area. This calls for a soft carbon pencil. If you used a harder lead or any lead here, the result would be a shiny mark. The lead pencil requires a little more pressure in its application than the carbon. This often tends to burnish the surface of the print and make a shiny spot. In retouching or spotting the lighter areas of the print, where only a faint line, spot, or shading is required, the harder lead pencils are used. The softer carbon used here would leave a black mark and would not blend in correctly. If you want to emphasize a light gray detail, but only slightly, a hard lead pencil will do this easily.

For retouching, a long point is necessary. It should be at least an inch in length, but points of two or even three inches are better. The long point enables you to see the area where you are working. With a short point, your view can be blocked by the wood of the pencil or the holder.

You can count on the retouching pencil to do simple spotting, to retouch and smooth faces, to blend and soften hard lines, and to strengthen details.

The Eraser

The pencil is only one tool. There are others that complement and supplement it. It is only logical that one of these should be the eraser. There are many types of erasers available. Most of these have a definite use for the photo-restorer or positive retoucher. There are very hard erasers, such as ink erasers, which can be obtained in pencil form and can be sharpened to a point. They are very handy for getting into small places or details. There are softer types of eraser, such as those on the end of a writing pencil. The softer types have a drawback, because the erasers soon wear down. You can get eraser tips that fit over the end of the pencil. These are very handy. Or you can get the same type of eraser in a three-inch stick, which can be cut by scissors into various shapes as needed. Then you have the Artgum or kneaded rubber erasers, which are very soft. Both are ideal for cleaning out wide areas. The kneaded one has the added advantage of being able to be molded into any shape.

The ink or hard-type eraser is useful for getting into and cleaning out small areas and pulling out finer details. The rubber type is good for cleaning wider areas and can also get into the smaller areas. The Artgum or kneaded eraser should be used for wide areas and general overall cleaning. It also can be used to lighten an airbrushed area to a slight degree, as it can remove just as much of the work as you desire without rubbing it all out. The eraser can be used to correct any mistake you may have made with the pencil, as well as pulling out highlights and raising details.

The Etching Knife

The object in using an etching knife on the print is to remove black spots. This is done simply by scratching or shaving at the emulsion of the print. Any piece of steel with a fine, sharpened point or edge can be used for this purpose. Now we can get rid of a black spot by scratching out the emulsion until the paper base is reached. But this will leave us with a hole in the print that we do not want. If we, instead of scratching or digging, shave away at the spot, we will gradually reduce it. If this is done correctly, there will be no hole. As the emulsion is removed, the spot goes with it. This requires a sharpened blade and an experienced hand. The shaving effect is the secret of etching on positive prints.

There is a variety of tools that can be adapted to do this job. This was mentioned in the discussion on copy negative retouching. The tools are the same. The scratch pen and holder is the easiest to use. The holder is comfortable to the hand and offers a maximum of control. A razor blade can do the same job but is harder to handle, and you run the risk of cutting your fingers. The hobbyist's modeling knives also can prove useful.

Etching is not only a matter of removing small black spots. You may have to reduce larger spots or want to lighten a shadow. Here you will need an edge, not a point. The diamond-shaped scratch pen comes to a point and, as such, is not very good for reducing larger areas. But the edge of the razor can do this, as can a modeling knife with a broader blade edge. Because of the need for a sharp blade edge, the scratch pen, the razor's edge, and the modeling knife have to be honed or sharpened on an oilstone as you work. The edge can be dulled after a few minutes' work and requires sharpening. On the diamond-shaped scratch pen, the effect of this is to wear away at the point and produce a broader edge. By keeping more than one holder and a number of scratch pens, you can have a collection of varying size edges for your different needs.

Crayons and Pastels

Crayon pastels come in black, brown, and other colors. Only the pastel-type crayons are useful to the photo-restorer. Wax-type crayons are no good. The pastel can be applied to the print by finger tip, a piece of chamois cloth, or with a tortillon stump. The use of the finger should be avoided unless absolutely necessary. Should your hands be moist or sweaty, this could damage your work. The chamois cloth is good when you desire to tone in a broad area. The stumps are good for getting into small spaces.

What can these pastels do for you? They are handy for toning down hot spots, shading, outlining a coat or dress that has to be built in, and shading this for a rounded effect. They are especially helpful with outline work, as the pastel can be worked out with the stump or chamois cloth to soften lines, so that when air-brush color is applied on top of it, it blends and does not show through as a hard line. A large, flat, too white area can be toned down with black pastel that is applied evenly with a chamois cloth. The highlights can then be pulled out with an eraser in order to create details or roundness. This method works well with white shirts or blouses as well as with some faces.

Much of the same work can be done with a pencil and stump. More than one tool can be used to do a certain job. Very few effects, it will be found, are the exclusive province of one particular tool. Which is the best? Which is most efficient? These are questions that only the individual working artist can answer for himself. Many artists will use the different means available interchangeably, depending upon the requirements of a particular job or even, unscientifically, upon the way they feel.

Spotting Colors

Most, if not all, spotting can be done with a retouching pencil. But there can be occasions when it may be necessary to use a spotting brush and spotting colors. Sometimes the pencil will not take on a certain paper surface. Commercial spotting colors are obtainable in photo or art shops. Regular water color can be used just as well. On black-and-white prints you can use black paint or opaque white. By using a piece of card as a palette, you can blend the black-and-white paints to obtain any intermediate shade of gray you require. However, moistening the spotting brush, fixing the point, and mixing the color takes time, more time than would be necessary to pick up the pencil and attack the spot. Here, too, however, the choice is yours. You may find that you like using spotting colors rather than retouching pencils. You should try both.

One special instance where the spotting brush can prove valuable is the case of a persistent black spot that will not yield to etching, for some reason or other. The black spot can be touched over with white or gray opaque spotting color to blend into the surrounding print area. Conversely, there may be a white spot in a very black area which cannot be adequately covered by lead or carbon pencil. Here, a dense black spotting color will do the job. And, if you want to duplicate a pattern or design when spotting out a crack or tear, the spotting brush with blacks, grays, and whites can prove much more facile than a pencil and knife.

Finally, in spotting colored or toned prints, spotting colors can be matched to the colors or tone of the print.

Tortillon Stumps

Tortillon stumps are compactly rolled sheets of paper that are formed into the shape of a cylindrical tube and come to a point. Their broadest use can be best described as one of spreading tone, or blending. They can be used to spread out and soften the lines made by charcoal, pastel, and pencil. They can also be used to apply a spot or line of pastel color or charcoal to the print. This can be especially helpful in toning or coloring lips and eyes on color restoration jobs.

Water Colors

Water-based colors are used, almost exclusively, in restoration work because they are the best type of colors for use in the air brush. They have the added advantage of being available both as transparent and opaque color. The former is important in tinting and in deepening a tone, the latter in covering. They are available in blacks and whites, grays, browns, and the colors of the spectrum, so they can be used on black-and-white prints, toned prints, and color prints.

The Air Brush

The air brush is the most valuable tool that the photo-restorer has at his disposal. It is also the most difficult to master. But, as has been noted before, without it, photo-restoration would be impractical. Its use, therefore, is a "must."

It is most valuable to the photo-restorer as a tool for applying paint or color to the workprint, to cover, to shade, to tint, to strengthen local areas, to get into finely detailed areas, to cover wide areas, and to do this with a smooth result that is photographic in appearance.

All this can be done because of the air brush is designed to apply color smoothly. When an area is airbrushed, there are no tell-tale pencil lines or hand brush strokes. Effects of roundness and depth can be obtained. Shadows and highlights can be worked out. Airbrushed artwork can be blended to match the rest of the print so that the picture is a whole unit and does not look patched.

We must mention the ability of the air brush to use paints that are either transparent or opaque. This is very important. The transparent paint or color can tone down a light spot or darken it without obliterating any of the photographic details. Thus an air brush can be used effectively and efficiently to tint or color a photographic print. Opaque

72. Workprint analysis.

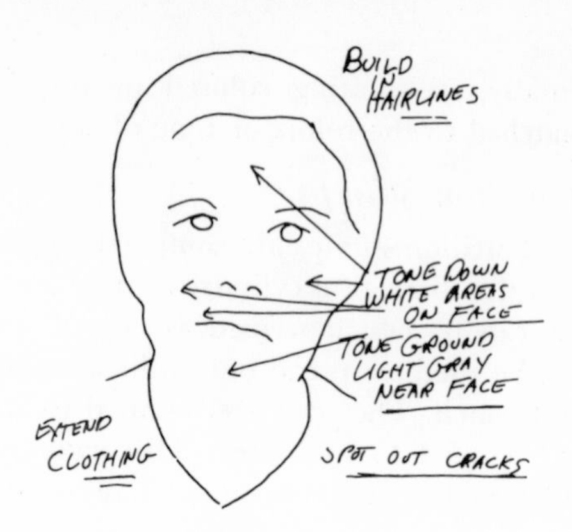

73. (BELOW) Workprint finished according to analysis instructions.

74. (ABOVE RIGHT) Background extended to edges by airbrushing. Shoulders finished and body mass built in by airbrush work.

75. (BELOW RIGHT) Further improvement made by darkening corners of ground by airbrushing and adding details to dress by airbrush detail and stencil work.

paint can cover any unwanted detail of the print and can be blended into the rest of the photograph or can be shaded and worked into some sort of a design or pattern.

This instrument is so important that a chapter devoted solely to its handling has been added at the end of the discussion on photo-restoration. However, for the purposes of this chapter we will just mention it and its use in positive retouching with the assumption that you know how to use it.

RETOUCHING AND RESTORING THE WORKPRINT

Retouching and restoring your workprint is not just a matter of sitting down at the easel or drawing board and starting to work. If you were to do that, you would never finish the job. You would soon find yourself bogged down and in trouble. If there were a teacher behind you or an instructor nearby, he could help you out. But, if you are working this problem out alone, you can soon be lost.

The only way to prevent this is to work out some sort of a blueprint or work plan. You must know what you want to do, what you are going to do, and how you intend to do it. You may not be able to follow such a plan to the letter. Something may come up that would necessitate a change in plan; in fact, something probably will. But, at the very least, this will guide you through the job.

Let us outline and discuss this plan briefly at first, before going into more detailed discussions.

First you should analyze the job. What does it require? What do you want to accomplish? What must be done? Then you must do some planning. How are you going to do what you want to do? What steps should you take? The following step-by-step procedure should be laid out; step one, the background; step two, the clothing; step three, the face. Such a procedure, working first on the background, then the clothing and, finally, the facial area, can be followed with most restoration jobs. However, it is not an absolutely rigid sequence. There will be numerous instances where it will be more expeditious to alter the arrangement. But, in the beginning, it will be a good idea to follow this.

In studying the background, you will determine how it is going to be treated. You will decide whether or not to retain the same background, retouching it, if necessary, whether or not to modify or improve it, and whether you should remove it entirely, rebuilding a plain one or adding one with some sort of a design.

When it comes to the clothing, you can either retain it as is or change it to something new or better. If you keep the same clothing, you may

76. (LEFT) *Background and clothing built out to edges of print by airbrushing.*

77. (RIGHT) *Final touches made by darkening outer edges of background, etching detail into hair, emphasizing collar by means of etching knife and cleaning face with airbrush opaque.*

find it necessary or desirable to make some corrections, such as removing spots, softening creases, or making the clothes appear neater and more modern. If you change the clothing entirely, you may do this by covering the original apparel by opaque, then drawing in the new clothing and then rendering it by air brush to obtain a photographic appearance. However, had you airbrushed the copy negative or vignetted the print, you could have had a workprint with only the head and neck showing, so that all you would have to do is draw in the new clothing and airbrush it. There is a tremendous savings of work here.

The face is more complicated. Work here must be done with the idea always in mind that the likeness or character must be retained. If the face requires no work, none should be done. The face should first be examined as a whole. Are there spots, blemishes, or cracks? Are there hard lines to soften? What is the best way to do this, pencil, knife, pastel, or airbrush?

Then each of the features should be checked. You can travel from the top of the facial area to the bottom. Start with the subject's hair. Does it require fixing? Should you clean up the outline and remove stray hairs? Should you tone down or raise highlights? Should hair be added to the top or to the scalp line? It is possible to be asked to add a complete head of hair, and this can be done.

Then you come to the forehead. Is it wrinkled? Do frown lines show? Should you remove or leave them? Then come the eyebrows. Do they need strengthening or shaping? Should they be left alone?

The eyes are of prime importance. We have to approach them with

78. (LEFT) *Subject cropped from group negative.*

79. (RIGHT) *Effect obtained by using the airbrush to tone down or "phantom" the background, to vignette the bottom and cover the head on the left.*

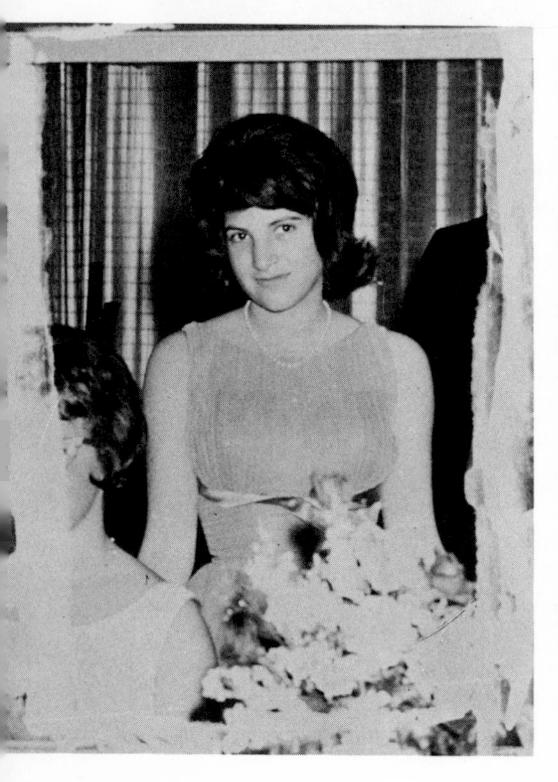

care. A wrong piece of work can change their aspect entirely. Very often the eyes are not critically sharp and the catchlights are not in the ideal place. Should the eyes be sharpened? Should you change the catchlight or put one in if there is none? Or should you leave the eyes alone?

Some person's ears are very prominent. Should they be toned down? Should they be cut down? With the nose, the first concern may be the nostrils. Should these be strengthened? Also, should the bridge of the nose and the tip or bulb be highlighted or brought out more?

Do the lips need sharpening? Does the chin need strengthening? Some subjects will have a mustache or a beard. Should these be strengthened or brought out more? Should they be made to appear neater or combed?

And overshadowing all is the question, "How will these changes or improvements affect the likeness?"

80. (LEFT) Workprint of ambrotype, illustration #34, with background made white by airbrush opaquing on the workprint.

81. (CENTER) Same workprint with blemishes on clothing covered by airbrush black.

82. (RIGHT) Finished workprint with face retouched, details brought out on clothing and white background toned down.

Once through these little steps, how are you going to review and check the work? What will the picture itself tell you? Should you compare it with the original? What should you look for? Or should you compare it with an unretouched duplicate workprint? How can you look at the likeness? How can you tell if you've retained it? If there appears to be a change, is this due to correction work, to retouching, or to a change in composition?

ANALYZING THE JOB

Each restoration job is different. Moreover, no two jobs will require the same treatment. Even if the originals are similar, there must be some difference in the work that you are going to do. Therefore, it is important that you have a good idea of what you want to do and of the results you expect to obtain in the finished workprint. Successful restoration work cannot be accomplished by merely advancing into the job and allowing the results to come out as they will. You must be the master of the job; you must not let it master you. Of course, it is very possible and it will often happen that you will not be able to get the results you want. But you will get closer to that goal knowing where you want to go than by not knowing. Planning the work, knowing what you have to do, and what steps you are going to take will make your work more efficient.

It should go without saying that to analyze the job and to decide what must be done, you have to study the picture. You should set out both the original and the copy workprint on the easel and study them, comparing one to the other. If you have made more than one workprint, pick out the best one for finishing. You can make notations on the other workprint to show where work is necessary and to serve you as a work guide. A transparent overlay can be used for the same purpose but will not prove to be as handy as a marked duplicate workprint.

There are certain things to look for. First, are there any faults with the original picture that must be removed? These faults are cracks, dirt, spots, stains, fading, missing parts, etc.

Secondly, are there any corrections or changes that can be made to improve the appearance of the picture? Here you should consider background modification, making clothing neater, and correcting facial blemishes. Since these corrections constitute a change from the original, you have to make a decision whether or not to do them. Sometimes the choice is not yours, as when the client requests corrections.

Thirdly, there are those changes and corrections that have been ordered or are necessary to the special nature of the job. New clothing, a new suit, dress, or tie could be requested. You may be asked to change the background. You may be asked to remove some blemish from the face or to remove a hat. If the job is one where you have removed a subject from a group for a solo portrait, building in parts of the body and changing the background to cover the parts of the surrounding people must be done.

CORRECTING THE FAULTS

Black Spots

Black spots can be removed either with the etching knife or by covering with air brush opaque white. They can also be eliminated by the utilization of a spotting brush and white paint. Thus you have three choices to get rid of a black spot, line, or scratch. One of these will prove to be the easiest for you. But the choice can differ with each job. What will be best for one particular job may not be the best for the next one.

When the spots are on the facial area, near the eyes, mouth, or another critical feature, it is best to use the etching knife to remove the spot or, if this does not work, the spotting brush. Correction of the exact local area of the spot is essential, so that the retouching does not interfere with or change the vital feature. When the air brush is used, the covering will tend to spread out and thus, while killing the spot, will dim part of the area surrounding it. You can lose part of an eye, the line of the mouth, or a nostril this way. But, if the spot is a large one, etching or the use of a spotting brush can take up too much time without smooth results. In such a case, especially on the background or clothing, you will find the air brush method better.

White Spots

White spots can be filled in by pencil, carbon or lead, depending upon the intensity of the area surrounding the spot. They also can be spotted in by air brush and black paint or can be spotted with a spotting brush, water color, or India ink. The nature of the job, or of the spot, will determine which of these tools would be the best to use. For one, two, or a few smaller spots, the pencils would do the job with the most efficiency. If the spot is in a very intense black area where the pencil does not take, the spotting brush will do the job. If it is a very big spot, it can be filled in by air brush in less time than it would take to pencil it in,

83. (LEFT) *Preliminary airbrush work to eliminate background and cracked caused by cutting and rejoining copy negative.*

84. (RIGHT) *Workprint finished building shoulders, rebuilding details in woman's arm and darkening the corners of the background. On this print, little or no facial work is necessary.*

and the result will be smoother. If there are a lot of small black spots, so many that it would take an eternity to spot them out by pencil or brush, it is better to eliminate them by covering them with air-brush color.

Stains

Stains will show up, with very few exceptions, as darker spots on the print. They will usually cover larger areas than spots. If the stain is on a print area that should be white or light gray, it can be removed by being covered with air-brush opaque white. In other words, it should be covered. But if the stain is on a darker print area, it can be blended into the surrounding area by pencil retouching along the edges, to kill the outline of the stain, and blending by tortillon stump or airbrush work. This would involve darkening the surrounding area to a tone equal to that of the stain area. These two methods can be used separately or together. As you do the job, and as you do more and more restorations, you will learn which is the easier or better method and which will provide you with better results.

Cracks

Upon examination, you will see that the crack shows up on the workprint as a series of black and white lines, dots, or spots. We have at our command several ways of removing or retouching these cracks.

One is to use the pencil or spotting brush to fill in and darken the

85. (LEFT) Workprint treated to cover hole in chest area, background airbrushed to cover cracks, cracks and spots removed from face by spotting and etching.

86. (RIGHT) Same workprint finished by darkening edges of background, lightening area near face to create a spotlight effect; bringing out details on insignia and cap braid with an etching knife and smoothing rougher areas on face by airbrushing.

white parts of the crack, while the black components can be reduced by etching. This will, in most instances, leave a sort of scar running through the print. This scar can be de-emphasized by further blending of the surrounding print area, by further retouching, stump work, or airbrushing.

Had the copy negative been airbrushed over the crack, you would have a white space or canal running through the print where the crack had been. The missing tones can be replaced and blended to the rest of the print by air brush. Missing details can be drawn in with fine air-brush work, stump and charcoal work, or by pencil retouching.

The crack, as shown on the workprint, can be covered with air-brush opaque of neutral color. This neutral color, white or gray, can be mixed to match, as closely as possible, the tone that predominates the area along the crack. Even so, this will leave a channel running through the print covering the crack. When the opaque is dry, details can be built in by air brush, pencil, or stump to blend in with the rest of the print.

The crack can also be worked out with a spotting brush and opaque paints, from white through gray to black. These colors can be applied and blended to obliterate the marks of the crack while working in the missing details.

Tears, Breaks, and Missing Parts

A tear in the picture, a break, or a missing part are similar in appearance to cracks and can be considered the same as cracks when it comes to retouching. The main difference may be that a large, broad area of the print may be missing and may need to be replaced or rebuilt, while the crack is only a sort of line running through the picture. This area must be rebuilt. This can be done by working it in with the air brush, with pencil, or black pastel, and stump work or by spotting brush with blacks, grays, and whites. The ragged boundary edge will have to be retouched and blended into the picture. This can be done by pencil and stump work, or the edge could be covered by air-brush opaque. This will provide a soft blending from the picture area to the missing area so that air-brush work can be done. The same effect can be obtained by airbrushing the copy negative over the area of the tear, break, or missing part so as to produce a whitened area on the workprint. The size of the area and the number of details involved will do much to decide which of these methods will be best for your use.

CORRECTIONS AND CHANGES

Corrections and changes are actually extra or in addition to restoration. The inherent damages and faults just discussed must be removed or touched up. There is no alternative. But corrections and changes are not necessary, and if there is a requirement for an "as is" restoration, it is not desirable. An "as is" restoration can be defined as one in which everything, every detail is retouched and rebuilt to re-create the picture to represent the original as it was when first made. In other words, it must be an actual reproduction. But once you change the size or format, as from an oval to square or rectangle, or change the tone, as from black to brown, you open the door to effect other changes that could improve the final aspect of the picture.

A license does exist for the photo-restorer to change and improve a photograph. The only times we can imagine an objection are when the original may be of historical importance, when the original photographer is famous, or when the client does not desire any changes made. But when the original photograph is, regardless of its material condition, a bad one, (*i.e.,* a poorly composed or lighted picture), and can be improved, the artist-restorer should make improvements. A perfect restoration of a substandard original will still be substandard. Perhaps, if the original photographer had the material and means for improvement that the restorer has, he would have made use of them. At any rate, whether or not the restorer does have the right to change and improve another photographer's original work, he *can* do so, and we are going to discuss the different methods the restorer can use.

In the chapter on making the workprint, we have already discussed cropping and vignetting as methods of improving composition. Now let us see what we can accomplish in this vein with positive retouching.

Corrections and Changes on Backgrounds

Backgrounds can usually stand improvement. While a background is not vital to the character or likeness of the individual subject, it can affect the over-all aspect of the picture. Very often backgrounds are ugly, uncomplimentary, and distracting. This is especially true with snapshots. You will also find that many of the cheaper type photos, such as automatic pictures, resort area postcards, or souvenir photos have painted backgrounds that may be all right for a novelty effect, but do not have any place in a portrait, nor do they have any artistic or pictorial value.

The use of the air brush allows you a lot of leeway with backgrounds, to the extent of removing them entirely and substituting or building in other ones if necessary.

When the background is too prominent, it can be toned down. This can be done by applying black water color with the air brush to darken and subdue the highlight areas of the ground. This will darken the ground and at the same time, bring out the figure or face of the subject. If enough color is applied to the background, it will cover all details and give you a completely black result, which is sometimes desired.

On the other hand, by using white opaque water color, the background becomes whitened with a foglike or phantom effect. Here, too, if enough color is applied, the opaque will cover all details and give you a white background.

A spotlight or halo effect can be obtained by darkening the outer edges of the print so that just the figure and the background immediately surrounding it is visible. (We noted how this same effect was obtainable while enlarging by burning in the edges of the workprint.)

A vignette effect can similarly be obtained by the use of white paint instead of black. (This too can be done by vignetting in the making of the workprint.)

If these four treatments are not sufficient and if they do not do the job you want, then you can remove the background entirely. Removing the background is a matter of covering it with opaque paint until it no longer shows. The best method of accomplishing this is by air brush. It is possible to cover a background by hand brush and heavy tempera colors or even heavy opaque oils. But this will take longer, the brush strokes will be very visible, and the figure will look as if it were cut out. Air-brush work will be smooth and can be blended so that there is no "cut out" effect.

It should be obvious that if we apply enough air-brush opaque color to the surface of the background, we will cover it. Should we want a light background, we can use white opaque. For a medium tone ground we can use opaque grays, while for a dark or black one, we can use black opaque.

In doing this work, it is important to protect the figure or the subject so that it is not covered by the air brush color (*i.e.,* so none of the color goes over onto the figure). This can happen because the color comes from the air brush as a spray and spreads. To keep the figure clean we can (1) cut out a frisket or mask that will shield the entire figure or (2) use a hand stencil. The hand stencil is a sheet of cardboard or celluloid that the air brush artist holds in his left hand and moves over various parts of the picture as a shield, while he works over the picture with the air brush in his right hand. With either of these two methods, there is always the chance, despite precautions, of some of the paint going over the figure. The paint should always be removed. You can do this either by erasing or by washing.

To remove the paint by eraser, the first step is to go over the entire figure with a very soft eraser, either Artgum or kneaded. The greatest amount of unwanted "sprayover" will be along the edges or outline of the figure. There should be very little, if any, in the center of the figure area. Any that is in the center can be easily cleaned off with the soft eraser. As you move closer to the outline, a firmer eraser, such as a rubber pencil eraser, should be used. It should clean out most of the color, except for that which is very close to the outline. When erasing near the outline use a very hard, ink type eraser with a fine point. It can get around the curves of the outline and pick up the residue of color that has been deposited there.

If too much of the paint has gone on to the figure, you may find that erasing will not be able to clean it all out. In this case you will have to wash out the figure. This is done simply with a small swab of cotton, moistened with water. You can wrap some cotton around the end of a toothpick or the pointed handle of a spotting brush in order to get into the small curves or details and work close to the outline.

Sometimes after washing, a residue of the unwanted color remains. Rather than repeat the washing process and wait for the print to dry again, the residue can be removed by an eraser. Similarly, sometimes after erasing, you can have a stubborn spot that won't leave. It can be taken out with a piece of moist cotton.

When this is done, you will find that you have a plain, blank background. You may want to create something more interesting and relieve the monotony of the plain ground. The use of lighter or darker colors and the air brush will allow you to add a cloud effect. With the aid of a stencil you can get a sketch effect. And, if you want, you can build in a new, designed background with the use of air brush, stencil, stump, pastel, etc.

Corrections and Changes on Clothing

When considering the clothing, we have the choice of keeping, and if necessary, restoring it "as is." Or we can also improve the existing clothing or replace it entirely with something different.

If we intend to keep the same clothing, the only problems that have

87. (ABOVE LEFT) *Vignetted workprint (see illustration #67) airbrushed to make background an even color.*

88. (ABOVE RIGHT) *Effect obtained by attempting to sharpen the face with pencil, knife and airbrush work.*

89. (BELOW LEFT) *To add a suit to the subject, the outline has been indicated by means of tortillon stump and charcoal.*

90. (BELOW RIGHT) *Same workprint with suit laid in by airbrushing. Note how outlines from illustration #89 show through the layer of airbrush work.*

91. Workprint finished with suit modelled by airbrush shading, details brought out by airbrush stencil work, and design added to tie by tortillon and charcoal. Note airbrush effect on background to relieve its monotony.

to be faced will be those caused by dirt, cracks, spots, stains, and the necessity to rebuild some missing part. These faults can be corrected as we have discussed earlier.

Improving the clothing is something else. This is actually a correction, not plain restoration. But as we correct the clothing we will remove any inherent faults, such as those mentioned in the preceding paragraph. While we are improving, we should retain the same style and type of clothing that the original subject is wearing.

What kind of improvements are we expected to make? First, we can straighten creased clothing. Second, we can retouch ill-fitting clothing so that it appears to fit properly. Third, we can make the clothing look neater.

The simplest way to press creased clothing is to cover it with opaque air brush color and blend this to match the rest of the clothing. In doing this, you must be careful not to have your result look like metal, instead of cloth. While you do get rid of creases, folds must remain so that the result looks natural. Creases can also be removed by retouching and blending with pencil and knife. The latter method should be used only when there are one or two minor creases to eliminate. When there are many, the air brush will be better and quicker.

A bad fit can be corrected by altering the outline of the garment. A shoulder can be cut down, a lapel can be straightened, raised, or lowered. If pants are too long, they can be shortened, if too short, lengthened.

Clothing can be made to appear neater merely by toning down the highlights of wrinkles, adjusting a shoulder line, adjusting a collar line, straightening the edges or outline.

Changing clothing involves the complete removal of the existing garments and the drawing-in or rendering of a new outfit. If the clothing has already been removed by blocking on the copy negative or by vignetting on the workprint, the artist will find a clean white area on the workprint for his artwork. If this has not been done, then the artist's first task will be to cover the existing clothing with an even layer of opaque color. The color should be white if the new clothing is to be light in tone. Darker gray can be used if the new clothing is to be darker in shade.

Drawing or rendering the new clothing requires some skill in artwork. It is a freehand process; you must be able to draw the suit or dress in question. To the restoration artist who can do this, drawing in new clothing is the best, and in fact, the easiest method of accomplishing the job. New clothing must fit. The position of the head, neck, and shoulders of each subject differs with each original. The new clothing must be drawn in to accommodate these varying positions. The neck and shoulder lines must fit in and look natural. A certain degree of flexibility is required. It can be most efficiently obtained with freehand drawing.

The utilization of the air brush in this process allows you to obtain a photographic effect, so that when the job is skillfully finished, it will be difficult to notice that the new clothing is not actually part of the photograph. The air brush enables you to finish this with a photographic effect.

A study of clothing styles must be made. You should have a men's fashion magazine as well as one for women on file. A scrapbook of period costumes also should be made up. This need only go back to the period of the Civil War, as photography only goes back that far. However, the majority of clothing corrections and replacements will be made on modern or recent originals. On the old-timers, the clothing will usually be retained as it is, since most of these were formal or studio portraits where the subjects dressed especially to have the picture taken. It is only rarely that you will be requested, for example, to add a dress to a lady in the style of the 1880's. If you are, you can look up the style in the library if you do not have a sample of it in your scrapbook.

In choosing the costume to add to a subject, choose one that is neutral, that is not radical or extreme in taste. Take men's jackets, for example. The single-breasted jacket with notch lapels has always been in style. The cut of the lapel and the width of it may have varied slightly from time to time, but the general effect or appearance of the jacket has been the same. On the other hand, a double-breasted jacket is dated. It is more practical, therefore, to add the former to a subject than the latter. If you were to add a sport shirt, you should add a plain neat one, rather than one with embroidery or an extreme design. Also, if you attire a woman in a simple dress or blouse, with a round or a vee neckline, you do not commit yourself to the style of any one period.

Most of the time, the new clothing will be added to bust or head and shoulder portraits. This eliminates concern with such details as skirt lengths, waistlines, sleeve styles, pants cuffs, etc., in most instances. However, if the subject is a full figure these have to be taken into account.

Adding a shirt and tie. Let's see how we go about drawing in a new suit, shirt, and tie. We will assume that the first step, that of old clothing being removed, has been accomplished, either by opaquing the workprint or the copy negative, or by vignetting while printing.

The next step is to find or determine the neckline with a pencil. This should be done with a light touch, so that the lead or carbon does not press into the paper and the line can easily be erased. Then you should determine the set of the shoulders, how they fit into the neck and their width. Then indicate the collar and add the necktie, either a bow or four in hand.

When these outlines satisfy you, they should be strengthened by the use of a tortillon stump and black pastel. Blend them softly so that no hard pencil lines show. With the stump and pastel, you can darken and blend in the shadow areas to obtain the effect of roundness and a third dimension.

When this looks right, it should be gone over lightly with air-brush color, taking care not to apply the color too strongly, especially if the shirt is to be light in tone or white. A hand stencil should be used to keep the color applied to the tie from spraying over on to the shirt. A sharp-pointed eraser can be used to pick out the highlights and emphasize the seams. If you want to make it look like a fancy sport shirt, you can use a pencil or stump to indicate some stitching.

To add a coat jacket, as well as a shirt and tie. Here, too, a light outline should be made at first with a pencil. The neckline should be located first, then the shoulder lines. These will differ from those we have discussed in the preceding paragraph, since the shoulder line formed by a suit jacket is slightly wider than and different from that formed by a shirt. Then, from the neck, draw two lines to indicate the separation of the jacket from the vee of the shirt. The jacket may be closed or open, as you see fit. This will give you your main lines and form the mass of the body and broad drawing outline. You can now indicate the collar and add the necktie, bow, or long tie. Indication of the sleeves should come next, then the outline of the lapels, and the line of the breast pocket. After this, the ouline is complete.

When these outlines satisfy you, they should be strengthened by the use of a tortillon stump and black pastel. They should be blended so that the hard pencil lines no longer show. While the shadow area should be worked in to give you the effect of roundness, do not attempt to darken the entire jacket area, because it will consume too much time and should be done by the air brush. If you want to give your jacket a tweed, stripe, or herringbone effect, stump work should be done. When the air-brush color is applied over this, the designs will show through.

After this is done and everything looks right, we can proceed with the use of the air brush. It is very important to check your drawing at this point. If anything does not appear to be right or if you have to make some correction or adjustment to your drawing, it should be done now, before the application of air-brush color.

Now with the air brush apply an even tone of gray over the jacket area to obtain the desired shade. The details and shading of the tortillon work will show through. Then work into the shadow areas with a fine close spray to increase the effect of depth and roundness. Using a hand stencil, sharpen the shoulder lines, bring out the lapels, breast pocket, and shoulder seams. The finishing touches can be done by stump or pencil to define and indicate buttons, button holes, etc.

When the suit is done, you will probably find that some air-brush color has strayed over on to the vee of the shirt area, on to the background and on to the face. The shirt area should be cleaned out with an eraser. This is why we have finished the jacket before working on the shirt and necktie. When the unwanted color is removed, the tie should be strengthened by fine airbrushing and the shadow of the collar lines applied. Finishing touches here should be done by stump or pencil. Any color that has gone over on to the background can be blended in easily by additional air-brush shading or opaquing. The face should be cleaned by the use of a soft eraser, making sure not to disturb the collar line.

Women's clothing. As with men's clothing, the first step is to put in the outline, shoulder lines, necklines, bodice, etc., of the dress or blouse you wish to add to the subject. It is important to make some sort of rounded indication of the bustline. However, this must not be too obvious. You do not want the subject to look like an overdeveloped glamor girl, nor do you want the clothing to look like a sack. Use good judgment. The apparent age of the subject has to be taken into account. An elderly lady will naturally require a different dress than a young girl will. It should be plainer and more dignified. There are no set rules or regulations. It is, in truth, a matter of experience and taste. (If the photo-restorer is a female, there should be no problem; if a male, he can always seek female opinion.)

After the apparel has been outlined, it should be emphasized and rounded with stump and charcoal. When this is done satisfactorily, the layer of airbrushing should be applied to obtain the desired tone of the clothing. Then the shadows should be strengthened and the figure rounded out. Details can be picked out by eraser, stump, or carbon pencil.

Full Figures

So far, the discussion of adding clothing has dealt with bust poses.

What about full figures? How do we proceed?

The procedure differs somewhat from that of working on a bust picture. In the first place, it is impractical to remove or bleach out the figure entirely, as we did with the head-and-shoulders portrait. This is because the job of redrawing the full figure would be a large one, as attention must be paid to arms, legs, hands, and feet, which is all very time-consuming. On the other hand, when making the workprint, the printer will have difficulty judging the proper head size and placing to allow room for the figure to be drawn in properly. A difference of one-quarter inch in head size could result in a dwarfed figure or a figure running off the print. Therefore, with the full figure subject, it is better to retain it as it is on the workprint and build the new clothing over it.

The outlines of the new clothing should be drawn in with a soft carbon pencil. With a man, as you add the jacket the shoulder line will be wider than shown by the shirt or overalls he may be wearing. The outline of the jacket should be added first, then the trousers, and then the shirt and tie.

Use the tortillon stump to soften the pencil lines. There will be some distracting highlights and shadows that are formed by the original clothing lying under your drawing. An attempt should be made to blend and retouch them to the new clothes. This could eliminate a great deal of opaque airbrushing. Some opaquing will be necessary, but it should be kept to a minimum.

A layer of airbrushing should be sprayed over the work. The air brush should also be used to blend and shade the old clothing into the new. Try not to allow your work to become too dark or black. When you have gone as far as you can in this manner, you can apply a layer of opaque airbrushing to smooth out the clothing. A hand stencil should be used constantly to keep color from going over on to the background or the face. However, if any does, leave it alone for the time being. It can be corrected after the clothing is completed by reworking the background. In such a case, there is no reason you cannot do the clothing first, then take care of the background.

Once you have this air-brush work laid in, details can be added by the use of pencil, stump, or the air brush and hand stencil.

While we may have the suit finished, the collar and tie still remain undone. We have left this for last because no matter what precautions we try to take we can anticipate a great deal of air-brush color going over on to the vee of the shirt, since it is a small space. Therefore, we will have to clean it out, either with a hard eraser or with a small piece of moist cotton. After this space is cleaned, the lines of the collar and the tie are indicated by pencil. The pencil work is softened by stump, and the air brush used to add some body to the tie and shadow of the collar. However, since this is apt to be small for air-brush working, you will have to depend more upon the pencil and stump to apply the finishing touches and details.

When working on new clothing for a female subject, you can anticipate more varieties in styling. Men's clothing, on the whole, follows the same lines through the years. But with women there will be differences in collars and necklines, cut of the dress, height of the hemline, etc.

It can be helpful, especially if you find that you have a number of calls for such clothing changes, to work up a stylish dress of neutral date and appearance. This should be something basic, so that by means of slight alterations and changes, you can fit it to the period or date of the subject.

Paste-Up Method of Adding Clothing

Obvious questions are, "Aren't there other ways besides drawing to add or change clothing? Can't we make use of other photographs?"

The answers are yes. We can use a picture or print of the desired clothing and paste it over the subject. If the original is large enough, that is; if it is not of miniature or snapshot size, the print can be pasted over the original before the first copying. Then the lines and hard edges, plus any misfitting, can be corrected when finishing the workprint. If the original is too small to do this on, it has to be done on the workprint. In this case, an additional copy step will be necessary. The print from the recopy negative becomes a secondary workprint, as the cutout edges from the paste-up will have to be eliminated here. If additional prints are wanted, this secondary workprint must be recopied.

Such a procedure involves collecting a file of clothing prints. The collection has to be extensive enough to fit the variety of subjects you may come across. Since the size of these prints cannot be expected to fit your original, you should make up copy negatives of each, from which you can make single-weight prints properly sized to fit the subject on the original or workprint, and which can be used for your paste-up. Such a file can be built up with time, or as each problem presents itself, by finding the desired clothing sample and saving it for the future.

Is this method superior to that of drawing in the clothing? Well, this depends upon the skills of the individual photo-restorer. As we have said before, photo-restoring involves skill in photography, retouching, and artwork. The complete photo-restorer must be a photographer, a retoucher, and an artist. It is conceivable that he will be more skilled in one of these than the others. If it is photography, he will try to do most of his restoring with the aid of photography, by copying and in printing. In his case, this paste-up method will probably be advantageous. If his strength lies in retouching, most of his restoring will be attempted by retouching the copy negative. If he is most skilled as an artist, he will rely mostly upon artwork and will find it easier to add clothing by drawing than by photography.

As far as time, in minutes and seconds, is concerned, the artist should be able to do his job quicker than the photographer. Picking the clothing print, copying and sizing it, cutting it out, pasting it, etc., involve a lot of time. As far as results, the photographer's should be more photographic. If the artist is good, however, his drawing should look photographic.

So the final choice becomes yours. You will have to learn which is easier for you and which provides you with better results.

Corrections and Changes on the Face

The most important part of any portrait photo-restoration is the face. In viewing and studying the face, we must examine the hair, facial outline, eyes, mouth, nostrils, eyebrows, mustache and beard if any, the set of the chin, wrinkles, and character lines. These make up the face. The face is a whole, a unit. It must be regarded as such. But it is made up of parts that relate to each other and make up the unit, and these must be taken into account. Any change that may be made to these parts by positive or air-brush retouching can cause a change in the likeness of the whole face.

A living face moves. But the face on a photograph is fixed in time and space. The relation of the parts, the tones, and the shadows create the illusion of the particular subject's likeness, character, and if the portrait is a good one, personality. If a change or correction is made here, it can have a damaging effect. But often such changes are necessary. When there are marks, stains, spots, scratches, or cracks on the face, retouching or removing these will create some change, if only that of the actual repair.

Very often corrections are requested. If you have to make the hair look neater, sharpen an outline, strengthen the eyes, soften wrinkles, or remove blemishes, here too some element of difference between the original likeness and that of the restoration must be created.

Despite this, after such corrections have been made, the portrait should still be of the same person, even though there may be local differences due to the retouching. In restoring or retouching the face of the subject, the retention of the likeness must always be kept in mind, and as you proceed with your work, you must continually check to see that you are not overworking or overretouching and straying away from the character.

Let's examine the face and its parts and try to see what work, if any, is required and how we are going to go about doing it.

First, let's take the hair. Are there ragged outlines that could be made neater? Are there stray hairs that should be removed? Should the highlights be brought out more or should they be toned down? Seemingly, this should not affect likeness. People comb their hair and change their hairdos, but still remain the same people. But we are not dealing with people, we are dealing with a picture. These corrections will make a change in the picture. Will that contribute to a change in likeness?

Then, let's look at the eyes. These are very important. In fact, they may be considered the most important feature of the face. Do they require sharpening? Very seldom are eyes critically sharp, especially when the original is not a studio portrait. It is a simple matter to sharpen them by penciling the pupil or etching the whites. But, if you do this, how will this affect the picture? Should you bring out a catchlight? Is there more than one catchlight showing? If so, should the extra ones be removed? If the subject is wearing eyeglasses, is there glare reflected in the lens? Should this be toned down? What about the eyelids? Should that line be emphasized or strengthened? Should the whites of the eyes be cleaned out or brightened? Should the eyelashes be brought out? These are things that can be done. But if you do them, you should know how they will affect the overall aspect of the picture. Sometimes sharpening the eye can change the entire character of the picture. Most times it will not. This is something for you to see and judge.

The lips are also very sensitive areas. The outer lines of the lips are seldom sharp, but blend softly into the face—that is, unless the subject has used lipstick. There will be a tendency to emphasize these lines and to sharpen them. This can change the expression of the lips and mouth unless delicately and carefully done. The smaller the face, the smaller the original, the more difficult this will be. Often you will attempt this and have to remove your work, maybe several times, until you obtain the right effect.

While the nose is not as delicate, if we can use that word, as the eyes or lips, it still must be treated carefully. Its shape is often delineated by the shape of the bridge and the shadows alongside it. Does the bridge of the nose require highlighting? Should the shadows along the sides of the bridge be strengthened? What about the nostrils? They usually blend into the shadow that forms under the nose. Should they be emphasized? Too much work can make the nose too prominent. How can you tell how much to do? You have to develop your judgment. The only way to do this is by working and gaining experience.

The chin also must be considered. This is a strong character determinant. Very often, because of shadows, the chin is obscure. Should the chinline be strengthened and brought out? There is usually a highlight on the chin. Should this be emphasized?

The cheekbones also have a determining effect on the character of the subject, or rather, of the picture. How well they show up depends upon the lighting. Sometimes the lighting rounds them out and de-emphasizes them. Sometimes the shading makes them too prominent. In the former instance, shading and highlighting can bring the cheekbones out more; in the latter, they could be toned down.

The ears are of minor importance. Usually they catch the light, and upon enlargement seem too prominent. Often they stick out too much. They can be toned down with no damaging effect upon the likeness or character.

The package that holds all these items together is the outline. If the picture is sharp, the outline should be a definite one and require no work. But when a picture is diffused, or where there is no contrast between the face and the background, locating and indicating the outline becomes important. The clear outline seems to exist on the original. Its presence is felt. But on the copy print it disappears and has to be found. The original must be studied closely to see where this line is or where it should be.

FAULTS IN THE FACIAL AREA

Bearing the above in mind, let's take a look at the faults that we are apt to find in the facial area. To begin with, there are faults that are due to the deterioration of the original. These include cracks, spots, stains, and fading. Then there are natural faults that are inherent to the photograph and to the subject. These are wrinkles, heavy shadows, bags under the eyes, age lines, pimples, blemishes, and scars.

Differentiation is made here between deterioration and natural faults, because, were the original in perfect condition, the deterioration faults would not exist, while the natural ones would. This leads us to the conclusion that while deterioration faults must of necessity be removed, the natural ones do not. If the original is a professional studio pose, the

92. How airbrush work on the print has corrected the effect of removing a crack by airbrushing the copy negative (see illustration #55).

photographer would have, in most cases, removed such natural faults by lighting and retouching. So with such originals we would not be concerned with them. However, with the informal, nonprofessional, and unretouched originals, the problems of natural faults and blemishes will be present.

Deterioration faults must be corrected. There can be no question about that. But natural faults may or may not be corrected. This becomes a matter of judgment on the part of the photo-restorer or one of choice on the part of the client. Nevertheless, we shall discuss the corrections of these faults. Whether or not they should be applied to the particular restoration job on which you are working will be up to you.

Deterioration Faults

Cracks. Cracks are common. They have the annoying habit of traveling across the eyes or mouth or some vital part of the face. Therefore, they must be worked out by pencil and etching knife only. You should

93. Analysis of regrouped workprint (see illustration #62).

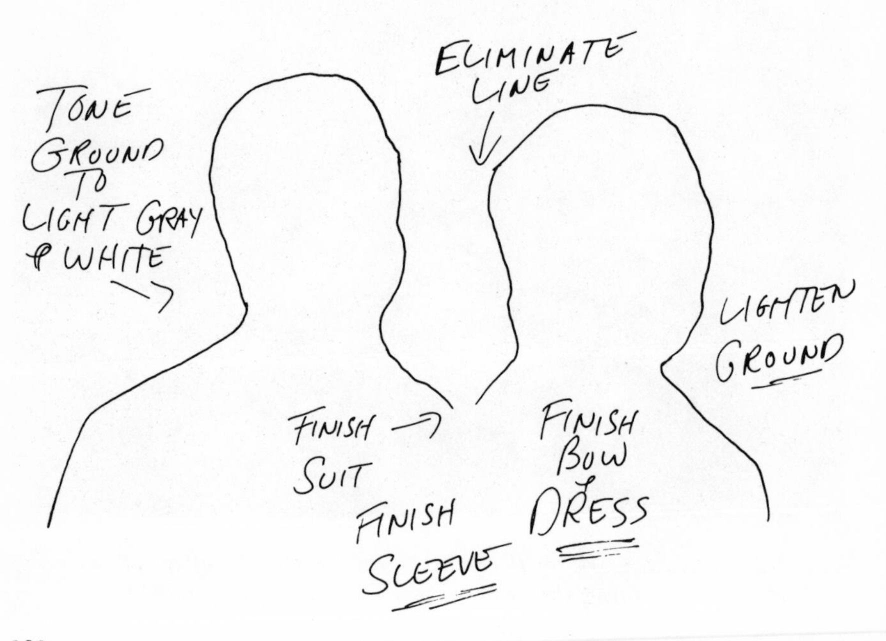

not attempt to work in air-brush opaque and then rebuild the whitened scar line. The pencil and knife provide you with extreme local control, which is very essential here. When retouching the crack where it crosses a vital feature, you must exercise care to restore the feature to its original appearance by following the lights and shadows and clues given you from either side of the crack. If a crack runs vertically through a face, it can have the effect of making it look longer; if it runs horizontally, of making the face appear wider. So, when you remove the crack, the difference will appear. The reason for it must be taken into account, therefore, when judging the work.

Spots. Spots, too, should be attacked with the retouching pencil or the etching knife. Since they often will form on or near vital features, extreme local control is necessary. A spotting brush, with black or white paint, can also be used. However, wherever possible, the pencil and knife are preferable.

Stains. Stains will cover a broader area than the spot or the crack. Where the latter will usually be rather definite as far as black or white is concerned, the stain may be of any shade from white, through gray, to

94. Workprint finished according to analyzed instructions.

black, depending upon how it registered on the copy negative. If the stain is a light one and details show through it clearly, removing it may simply be a matter of blending the edges of the stain into the rest of the print. This can be done with retouching pencil, knife, or tortillon stump. If necessary, the area surrounding the stain can be darkened slightly with the air brush to match the darker tone of the stain. If the stain should be lighter than the rest of the print, the reverse is true, and you darken the stain area.

But heavier and darker stains cannot be worked out as simply as this. Because of the larger area covered by the stain, it cannot be lightened or removed by an etching knife, as we would remove a black spot. We must resort to air-brush work. Opaque white or light gray is applied to the spot until the tone of the stain area matches the surrounding portion of the print. This use of opaque, however, will obliterate or subdue some details that may have been visible originally beneath the stain. These details then, must be rebuilt. The "stop-and-go" method can be used here. This method consists of opaquing the stained area lightly, so that the details underneath do not entirely disappear. Then the details are strengthened by going over them with pencil or tortillon stump, or by removing the covering paint locally with a hard eraser. Since the stain has not been lightened sufficiently, more opaque is applied and the details, once more, worked out. These steps may be repeated until the stain has disappeared. The alternative to this is to kill the stain entirely and then rework all the details with artwork.

Fading. When the face is faded, details are faint and the features are flat. Increasing the contrast is accomplished by making the shadows darker and emphasizing the blacks. In opposition, the highlights must be brought up. The use of opaque white to bring up the highlights may not be necessary. The darkening of the shadow and gray areas often eliminates the necessity for this. The use of an eraser here will bring out the highlights. There is usually a slight residue or sprayover to give the eraser some tooth. While the highlights may not actually be a pure white, they will seem so because of their relation to the darkened grays and strengthened shadows, and will be so on a properly made recopy print. You will find that most of the time, in treating this condition, darkening the black and gray shadows and darker areas will be sufficient to bring out the lighter areas without having to resort to white opaquing.

Natural Faults

Now let us examine the so-called optional retouching or correction work to the natural faults.

Wrinkles. Wrinkles show up as black lines or shadows on the lighter flesh tone. The high ridge of the skin fold may show as a highlight, lighter than the predominant flesh tone. They can be modified by the use of an etching knife to lighten the dark folds of the wrinkled skin, while a retouching pencil can tone down the lighter ridge. You can soften and tone down these wrinkles, in this manner, or you can remove them entirely. If you do the latter, you can find yourself with a portrait of an elderly person with very young skin, which will be greatly out of character. You have to use some judgment here. Removing wrinkles is not the same as softening them and making them less conspicuous. Removing them is too radical a correction. They should be toned down only to remove the apparent disfigurement but something must be left to indicate the subject's age.

Heavy shadows. Heavy shadows may be found on snapshot originals. If the original is a professional job, we can presume it was properly lighted and that, if there are heavy shadows, they were made on purpose. With the snapshot, however, it will often be desirable to lighten these shadows. They should not be removed entirely. They do serve to delineate contours and to emphasize facial features. Should they be eliminated, the contours can be lost and the features flattened.

Treament of these heavy shadows should have been anticipated by doing work on the copy negative or by dodging the workprint. On the copy negative, the shadow area could have been held back, or intensified, by the local application of a red dye or the careful application of airbrush color, diluted thin enough to carry no grain. Of course, the negative should have been large enough to allow such work to be done. In printing, careful dodging of the shadow area would have reduced or lightened the shadows.

If this has been done, the positive retouching requirements may only be to soften the hard line between the shadow and lighted areas and to strengthen or emphasize whatever details may have been dulled or softened. But, if this has not been done, you have a greater problem. How can you lighten the heavy shadow on the workprint? Remember, to lighten the shadow you have to get out the black, which is actually developed silver grains embedded in the emulsion. This is done either by etching or by covering it with white paint.

We have seen that we can get rid of a black spot or a black line by etching. Here we have only a small area to deal with. While it is theoretically possible to scratch out or shave off the larger area of a shadow, this method will take much time, require a great deal of patience and care, and, therefore, is impractical.

95. (ABOVE) *Workprint from portion of group photograph, intended for a portrait of the bearded gentleman by himself.*

96. (BELOW) *New workprint made after doing airbrush work on copy negative to eliminate background and boy covering man, thus saving much airbrush work on the workprint.*

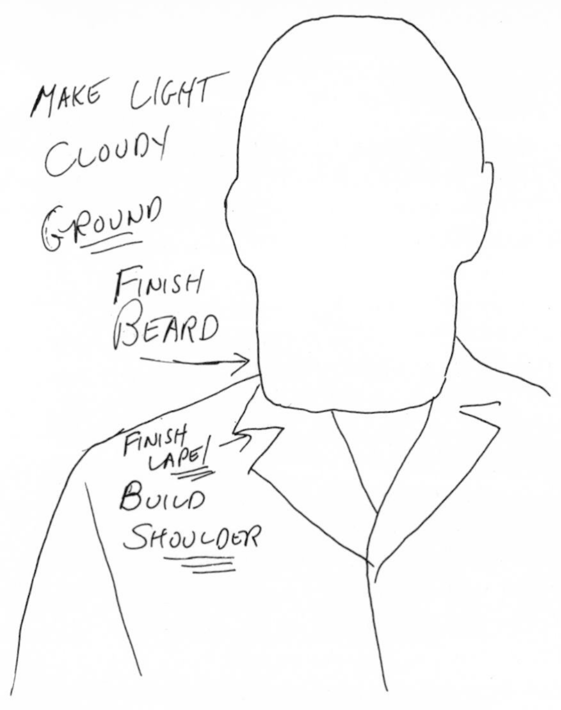

97. (ABOVE) *Workprint analysis or instruction sheet.*

98. (BELOW) *Workprint finished according to instructions.*

The use of a hard eraser, such as the ink eraser, will remove some of the blackness by the simple process of abrasion. You have to rub hard and use elbow grease. It can work if there was not much hardener in the fixing solution when the print was made. However, like etching, this method is impractical. Control is poor, and you can end up by tearing the paper or scratching it.

The best method is the use of air-brush opaque white. This means that you will have to recopy the workprint for final results, as the opaqued areas will have a blue-gray cast that is objectionable in a finished photographic print. The first step is to apply a layer of the white opaque to the shadow area in question. The paint should be on the thin side, so that it does not cover too thickly and is not grainy. Thus the primary application will be a light one, which will not hide any of the details that may exist in the shadowed area. These details should then be strengthened and brought out through the white layer. This can be done with an eraser, which will remove the paint that covers the detail. This method is better than using a stump or pencil, since it brings back the print detail itself and provides a more natural result than a rebuilt detail. The process should be repeated until you have lightened the shadow to the desired degree. It is a step-by-step stop-and-go method and can be stopped when you feel you have obtained the result you want. Some shadow effect should remain. It should not be removed entirely, although this is possible.

As stated before, the lightened shadows will have a bluish tone, which has been described as ghostlike, unnatural, or powdery. This, however, will become a natural tone on the recopy print. You have to learn to judge how the workprint will recopy. This takes experience. The blue-gray tone that appears a little too dark to the eye may copy on the light side. It is hard to set up rules or guides; your eye must judge. Photo-restoring is something that has to be learned by working. This book cannot do the job for you; it can only help by trying to show the way. However, even the experienced artist expects to do a little touch-up work on his recopy prints to correct any misjudgment of a heavily opaqued workprint.

Bags under the eyes. A properly lighted photograph should reveal no heavy bags under the subject's eyes. A professional portrait original should have been corrected or retouched to eliminate any that might have been caught by the camera. But most amateur and informal pictures (candids, nightclub shots, publicity shots, etc.) will need correction work in this area.

Whenever possible, the etching knife should be used. The eyes are an extremely critical area as far as likeness is concerned. The knife gives you absolute local control and you can get into the exact spot you want. Rarely should you attempt to use the air brush to cover these shadows. There is always the possibility of the spray carrying over on to the eyes and obscuring some vital little detail. The air brush should not be resorted to unless absolutely necessary.

Remember to leave some shading. Do not wash the shadow out entirely; some indication of depth must remain. Otherwise, the area below the eyelid will run into the cheek and give the face a blank or masklike appearance.

If the knife cannot be used or will not do the job, for some reason, try using a fine spotting brush with white or gray opaque. If you do have to use the air brush, apply the opaque as a fine dot, series of fine dots, or a line. It can be controlled in a small area. There will be a sprayover, no matter how carefully you work. Look for this. It should be cleaned off with a soft eraser or washed out with a pointed swab of moist cotton. Whatever goes on to the cheek below will be unnoticeable and have no effect upon the job.

Age lines. Age lines can be treated the same way as wrinkles. Here too you should remember that complete elimination of such lines may make the face appear too young for the subject.

Pimples and blemishes. Pimples and blemishes should be eliminated. They are actually temporary skin conditions and are not a component or important contribution to the likeness or character of the subject. (An exception to this may be a mole.) These are best removed by pencil and knife. However if there are many pimples, it may be more advantageous to air-brush opaque them. This will leave a very smooth skin on the subject. However, such pimples are mostly characteristic of young people, whose skin should appear naturally smooth.

Scars. Small scars that do not contribute to the character can be eliminated or softened in the same manner as wrinkles or age lines. But some scars are an important feature of certain people. While removing the scar will reveal the subject as he would have looked had he not been scarred, no one will remember him that way. Without the scar, his appearance is changed and there is an apparent loss of likeness. In this case, the scar should remain. It can be softened or toned down so that it is not the most prominent feature showing. Judgment is required here.

When the scar is a disfiguring one, such as a harelip, and creates an ugly or even horrifying visage, which may be emphasized by the enlargement of the restoration or the strengthening and building up of the print, it should be removed. Since most restoration work is done commercially at the order of a client, the client should be consulted and advised about the removal of such a disfiguring scar. Removing this is bound to change the face. Since the scar itself has changed that face from its natural appearance, the removal should, in theory, bring the face back to what it should have been. Here, too, judgment is needed. The scar may be toned down, softened, or de-emphasized, instead of being entirely removed. This may eliminate the ugliness without making too radical a change.

IMPORTANT FACIAL FEATURES

Now let's pay some attention to the eyes, lips, and nostrils, which are, perhaps, the most important details contributing to the individual likeness of a subject, as shown on the original photograph. In dealing with likeness, the basic rule all photo-restorers try or should try to follow is not to touch or change features. But this is not always possible. It is possible only when the original is a clear, sharp picture without blemishes that mar the features, although when this is so, the picture requires copying only and not restoration. So we find that except for a minority of cases, the features must be retouched, strengthened, or worked on to some extent.

It may be a good idea, at this point, to make a distinction between the likeness of the subject himself in life and the likeness of the subject as portrayed by the photograph or original. When we copy or restore a photograph, we are reproducing the likeness of the photograph, not of the actual person. Insofar as the original represents the actual subject, so will the copy restoration. In other words, the picture shows the way the subject appeared to the camera at the instant the shutter snapped.

It is logical to assume that when we have to change some facial feature, for either restoration or correction, we are going to effect some change in the face, some difference in aspect from the original. Putting on a new article of clothing, changing the shoulder line, or even making a lighter or darker background can often have a similar effect. All this should be remembered when we start to work on a face.

The Eyes

When the eyes are soft, out of focus, or diffused, they will seem to swim or be vague on the workprint, especially if the workprint is much larger than the original. There will be no sharp lines, dots, or catchlights to define the eye.

The eye is made up of the pupil, the iris, the white that surrounds it, the eyelid, the fold above the eyelid, and the eyelashes. It has a relation to the eyebrow, the tear gland, the fold or bag below the eye, and the bridge of the nose. On a sharp print with a fairly large head, these will show quite clearly. But, on small heads or diffused originals, these details are lost, do not show, and are only softly indicated or hinted at.

To add snap or life to the eyes, we can emphasize the catchlight, which often disappears in copying or enlarging, or may only be suggested in the original. Without this catchlight, the eyes look blank and can be described as "blind." This also holds true for the whites of the eyes, which also often disappear or fade into the shadow of the eye socket, leaving a black shadow instead of a delineated eye. By bringing out the white and the catchlight, the eyes and the face are rendered more lifelike.

The eye is framed by the upper and lower eyelids. Often on an original or on the copy print the whites fade into the lower lid while the upper lid is diffused. There is a compulsion on the part of the artist to take the pencil and strengthen and sharpen them. This can make the eye look artificial. Any emphasis on the division between the eye and the lid below should be very faint. The same is true for the fold above the upper lid. If this line is indicated, it should be done very softly. The line should not be made too definite, unless such a definite line shows on the original.

While attempting to sharpen or strengthen the eye, care must be taken not to overemphasize the retouching. A line or a dot in the wrong place, or applied too strongly, can change the look or likeness of the eye. Any degree of emphasis must be equal to the degree of sharpness of the photograph. We will find faces with varying degrees of clarity or focus. We will find that we must try to sharpen features on the blurry ones and that we cannot keep from touching these faces in accordance with the basic axiom mentioned before, "do not touch the face." This is because certain incongruities will appear as you work. For example, if you add new clothing, the work here may be sharper than the face. So, even if you had determined not to work up the face, you cannot leave it alone. After all, a picture is not merely a collection of separate parts put together in one print. It is a complete unit and must be viewed as such. One part relates to another and this relation must be realistic. So, in such cases, you are forced, in order to get a believable job, to sharpen the features to some extent.

Other Features

In addition to the eyes, sharpening will affect the nose and nostrils, the mouth and lips, the chin, and the outline of the face itself.

Anatomically each of these features has much in common and can be classified. But the human face is such that despite the billions of people on the earth each face is different from the others. No two are exactly alike. So, no two noses are alike, no two mouths are the same, etc.

Let's examine these features.

The Eye:	Pupil	Tear gland
	Iris	Lower lid
	Whites	Area directly below
	Upper lash and lid	
The Nose:	Bridge	
	Nostrils	
	Bulb	
The Mouth and Lips:	Mouth line	
	Upper lip and bow	
	Lower lip	
	Corners of mouth	

When examining the face on the workprint, before working on it, you should examine the above-mentioned features. You should try to determine whether or not they require any retouching, strengthening, or correction, or if they can be left alone. Also, you should have an idea of how much will be needed to strengthen them.

This work can be done by pencil, spotting brush, eraser, etching knife, stump, or air brush. A catchlight can be pulled out with the knife, as can the whites of the eyes. The lashes and lids can be emphasized by pencil if the head is a small one, or by stump if it is a larger one. A pencil dot can bring out the tear glands, while the shadow can be strengthened by fine air-brush work.

The bridge of the nose can be raised or highlighted with a fine-pointed eraser. A touch of the knife can highlight the bulb of the nose. A little pencil work, or stump work, can bring up the nostrils.

The mouthline, between the lips, can be emphasized by pencil work. The lips may be darkened slightly by the stump. The outline of the lips cannot be made sharp or they will look artificial, as if they had been made up with lipstick. On women this will show on the original, so no problem will be created. But on men's lips, or on those of women who use no lipstick, a sharp outline will change the mouth.

The shadows at the corners of the mouth can be deepened by pencil

99. Workprint (see illustration #71) finished by a minimal amount of airbrush work.

or fine stump work. These corners are important. They can make the mouth frown or smile. You can experiment by making the shadow lift, by raising it with pencil or stump shading, and by seeing how it makes the subject seem to smile or look more pleasant. The reverse will be true if you make these shadows droop. When you have the shadows drooping and making the subject seem to frown or look unpleasant, lightening or softening them will do away with the suggestion of frowning without changing any likeness.

This work should be done slowly. You should feel your way as you proceed. It will be easy for you, for example, to draw an anatomically perfect eye where it should be. But such an addition will not do, as it will not be the eye of the subject. Instead, you have to hint at or suggest the eye, or the nose, or the mouth, so that the improvement looks as if it is actually part of the photograph and not artwork.

When a face is badly blurred, much sharpening will be necessary. As you check your work the finished job must give you the feeling that your finished product is the same person as the one shown in the blurred original. Retouching is not precision work. You cannot get results by taking accurate measurements to achieve reproduction. This is visual art. You have to go by what you see and feel.

Such cases are extreme ones. It is advisable to avoid great enlargement with blurred originals. The size of the workprint should be kept small. A 3¼″ or 4¼″ or 4″ x 5″ workprint will be better than an 8″ x 10″ workprint.

In intermediate cases, where the original is not critically sharp, but slightly out of focus or diffused, an indication of the prominent feature details we mentioned will often be sufficient to do the job. You will have to know when to stop. This will come with experience. If you go too far, you will see it or feel it. There is always the temptation for the artist to proceed further in the search for a perfect portrait. With the original material supplied for most restoration jobs, a perfect portrait is not possible.

JUDGING THE FINISHED WORK

When you feel that the job is finished, or that you have gone as far as you can, it is time to sit back and review your work. Just what have you done? Just what have you accomplished? How do you go about checking the job? Just how do you criticize it? What standards should you use?

Self-criticism is very important to the photo-restorer. You can always get criticism from others. Such criticism will vary. But of what value is it? You have to be able to evaluate your own work. It must not be accepted blindly. If you feel you are right and the critic is wrong, you must be able to defend yourself. This is not so true in the case where you receive a general opinion, either good or bad, as when there is a specific point that brings comment. If you did something, made some change or correction, for a definite reason, you should be able to defend what you did and why you did it. You should be able to distinguish between informed, constructive analysis and uninformed opinions or flat statements of like or dislike.

Now this is not to suggest that you should reject criticism or ever get the idea that your work is above it. But there is criticism that should not be directed at restoration work. Criticism should be directed at the work of restoration, retouching, and correction, not at those elements that are beyond the scope of this work. Criticism of composition, posing, lighting, or expression, which are components of the original photograph, have no bearing on the restoration work.

When you look at your finished job to judge it, it is a good idea to step back and view it from a distance, so that you can see the whole picture as one, without directing your attention to any specific part. Does the picture hold together? Are the background, clothing, and face compatible? If not, why? In this viewing, if anything is glaringly wrong, you will notice it.

Comparison with the original is important. How close to the original is the restored copy? Does it differ in any respect? If so, why? This "why" must be analyzed. Is this difference due to a necessary correction or change that was made? Most often it is. If so, this difference is not only necessary but logical. If you change or remove a background, can the copy look the same as the original? If you retouch a torn cheek, or remove a crack that passes through a lip or eye, shouldn't you expect the repaired cheek or lip to look different because of the correction? In life doesn't a person often look different when dressed in formal clothes than wearing work clothes? If this is true in life, shouldn't it also hold true in a photograph?

However, the appearance or character of a picture, or its subject, can be altered by overworking or overretouching. If this is the reason for any difference, then you have to remove, re-do, or soften the part that is at fault.

If any original is very small in relation to the enlarged finished workprint, comparison will be difficult. An enlarging glass will be helpful. But the best and easiest method of comparison would be the use of another enlarged print, an unretouched guide print. This comparison will be revealing.

It is basically a matter of looking at your work, studying it, comparing it, and asking yourself questions. As you do this, the answers will come. Remember, most of the criticism must be self-criticism. Outside, professional, constructive, and instructive appraisal is important. The best source of this would be a more experienced photo-restorer or a professional photographer who handles photo-restoration work.

When you are satisfied with your job, the finished workprint should be sprayed with a fixative or lacquer to protect the artwork and prevent it from being rubbed or damaged by normal handling.

CHAPTER 7

RECOPYING

There are several purposes for recopying the air-brush retouched workprint. In the first place, we should consider the appearance or aspect of the artwork. The finished workprint often will show the signs, or scars, of the artwork. The etching knife, in scraping away at the emulsion, can leave an indentation that is visible when the picture is viewed from the side or at an angle. The lead pencil can leave a shiny spot, also readily visible from a side angle. (Note: These shiny spots are not visible when viewed directly from the front.) The air-brush work itself may either show as a matte or a glossy area, depending upon the type of paint or color that was used. Such matte or glossed areas do not match the remainder of the print. Also, whenever opaques, grays, or whites are used, the workprint assumes a bluish cast, which has no effect on recopy prints, but does give the workprint an odd, ghostlike, or disturbing appearance.

Recopying and making new prints will overcome these "faults" of the workprint. The vestiges of artwork and discoloration of the air-brush colors will not show on the recopy prints.

Another consideration is the variety of paper surfaces and tones that are available to make up a portrait print. The workprint is limited to a black-and-white, smooth-surfaced stock. We want no grain, we need no tones. But our finished, final prints are not so limited. Surfaces vary from very rough to smooth. Tones vary from warm to cold; there are sepias, goldtones, selenium tones, buffs, etc. The use of special papers and toning will provide finished prints of better quality and appearance than the air-brush workprint. Their use will improve the aspect of the restoration job.

Special papers are made for toning. If they are desired, you must have a recopy print. The finished air-brush workprint cannot be toned, as the immersion in the solution will wash off the artwork. You may desire to color the finished restoration with hand or brush oils. Coloring can help liven and improve a restoration. You should have a fresh recopy print for coloring. You can attempt to add the color to the air-brush workprint. This, however, can ruin the restoration work by rubbing or streaking and the results will seldom be as good as if you worked on a fresh print.

Size also is a consideration. We have found the 8″ x 10″ print the most convenient for finishing and artwork. But this does not necessarily have to be the most desirable size for the final print. Larger or smaller sizes may be wanted.

Once the workprint is recopied and a good negative is made, the final recopy prints can be made in any size. There is no restriction. There is also no restriction on the number of prints that can be made from that negative. Often duplicate restorations are wanted. It is ridiculous to make more than one restoration workprint, with all the extra work that would be needed. It is more logical to recopy that workprint for the duplicates or additional prints.

For these reasons, recopying is a necessary and essential part of the photo-restoration process.

COPYING

Copying the finished workprint is no different from copying any other photograph. In fact, it should be simpler. For one reason, no pre-copy work is required. This has been taken care of by the restoration. Nor should there be any need to take special care to eliminate grains, stains, or discoloration. All that is required is straight copying.

There should be no need to build up any contrast on the copy. The workprint contrast should be adequate. There may be an occasional instance where it is necessary to finish a workprint so that it is flat and without contrasting blacks and whites. In such an instance, a contrast film that will build up the copy is in order. Normally an orthochromatic film that will retain your halftone values, as well as the blacks and whites, should be used. Filters are not necessary.

PRINTING

Making your final restoration prints is a normal printing or enlarging

100. Typical finished workprint.

101. (LEFT) *Preliminary copy negative (see illustration #25).*

102. (RIGHT) *Recopy negative made from workprint #100.*

103. (BELOW) *Final print, showing improvement made by recropping.*

104. (ABOVE) *Final print, showing improvement made by vignetting and adding a little artwork to the background.*

105. (BELOW) *Final print, showing improvement that can be made by burning in the corners.*

106. Improvement that can be made by printing with an oval mat.

107. Effect obtained by using a roughly textured printing paper.

procedure. It should be simpler than making the workprint, as there should be no need for dodging, vignetting, or burning in. You can take advantage, however, of the recopy printing step to further improve or modify your work and to make the restoration job more presentable and appealing. This can be done by such means as recropping or recomposing, diffusing, using rough and textured papers or texture screens, toning, positive retouching, tinting and coloring, mounting, and framing.

Recropping and Recomposing

It is true that you did, or should have done, some cropping and composing when making the workprint. Sometimes, as in the case of a bust from a very small original, you could not bring up the head to the size you want. In making the recopy print, you can crop the picture to offer a larger head size. In the case of a full figure, you may find the feet and the lower portion distracting or objectionable. Here improvement can be made by cropping the final prints as three-quarter figures.

Diffusing

We should have been very careful, when making the workprint, to keep it as sharp as possible. This we found was essential. But the final prints might be improved if softened a little. Roughness from pencil retouching, etching marks, or air-brush grain that may show will vanish with a slight bit of diffusion. This should be used only if it will serve to make an improvement. It should not be relied upon to cover sloppy restoration work. It should not become a crutch. It is useful mainly with larger heads or bust shots. With groups or full figures, this can cause a loss of the finer details that are important to the picture and should be avoided.

Rough and Textured Papers

The use of a pebble grain, silk, rough, or canvas-textured printing paper will also act in the same way as diffusing, but without losing sharpness. The texture of the paper will camouflage any residue of the retouching, etching, air brush, grain, etc., especially with those full figures or groups that we could not diffuse. Textured paper offers a richer look and finish than the smooth stock we used for the workprint.

Texture Screens

Texture screens can be used to obtain the effect of an etching. They will really camouflage and hide any residual retouching marks and grain. Here, too, you should not allow the use of such a screen to become an excuse for doing less work than necessary on the workprint, with the idea that the texture screen will cover any lack of retouching. Keep in mind that not everyone will like the effect of this screen on the restoration.

Toning

Toning is valuable, especially when an original is yellow with age, is warm in tone, or is a brown tone. Very often a black-and-white print compared with these originals appears too cold. A bit of warmth added to the reprint will improve the job. The goldtone or sepia print looks much richer than the black-and-white one. There is no reason why you should not make toned reprints when the original is black-and-white. The improvement, by toning, can also make the difference between a passable job and a good one.

Positive Retouching

Additional work can be done on your recopy print. There will always be the necessity for a little spotting, as there is on any print. Also, the artist may notice something that he had not caught in the workprint or something that should be improved. Positive retouching can be done with the aid of retouching pencils, spotting brushes, etching knives, charcoal and stump, oil, or air brush.

Tinting and Coloring

Your recopy prints can be tinted with light oils, colored with heavier oils, or colored by air brush. This is in addition to the restoration work, but a good coloring job can turn an ordinary restoration print into something exceptional.

Mounting

Mounting is important in dressing up the finished picture. The recopy prints should either be placed in folders or mounted on mat boards before being presented to the client.

Framing

Framing is the final touch. Small restoration prints can be placed in metal or wood miniature frames. For wall frames or standing easel frames for the top of a dresser or shelf 8″ x 10″s can be used. Larger sizes should go into wall frames. When framed, your finished restoration will be displayed; unframed, it may disappear into a dresser drawer.

CHAPTER 8

THE AIR BRUSH

The air brush is such a vital tool to the photo-restorer that it merits its own chapter. As has been stated earlier, without this instrument photo-restoration would be impractical, if not impossible.

What is the air brush? What does it do? Why is it so valuable to the photo-restoration artist? To put it simply, the air brush is a paint sprayer it applies paint or color to the surface of the picture by means of spraying. Since the surface is of limited size, the spray of the air brush has to be selective. The air-brush artist wants to be able to make a fine line with his tool, as well as create a broad tone and light or heavy shading. The air brush he uses has to be able to let him do it. So the tool must be more refined and more complicated than the commercial spray gun that is used to paint large areas, such as walls or cars.

There are several brands of air brushes that are made specifically for this purpose. Naturally, each one has different features. However, in general, there is much similarity. Our discussion, therefore, will be in general terms as far as features and working parts are concerned. Specifications of each brand can be supplied by the manufacturer.

The air brush is not self-sufficient; it cannot work by itself. It requires a source of compressed air in order to create the spray. This can be supplied by a tank of compressed gas or by an air compressor. For the occasional operator, a tank will be sufficient. For the frequent user the compressor will become a necessity. A length of flexible hose is required to connect the air brush with the source of compressed air.

COMPONENT PARTS

The main components of the air brush are (1) the main casing or housing; (2) the hose connection; (3) the main lever or control; (4) the tip or spray regulator; (5) the color container; (6) the needle; (7) the handle. Mention must also be made of the two main channels: the air channel, which leads the air from the hose coupling to the tip, and the color channel, which brings the color from the cup to the tip.

The main casing is the body of the air brush. It is a hollow metal cylinder that contains the air channel, the color channel, and the needle, and to which the necessary component parts are attached. It is the heart of the air brush.

The hose connection is usually attached to the bottom of the main casing. It contains the air-valve mechanism that admits the compressed air to the air channel.

This valve is actuated by a downward pressure of the main lever.

108. Basic airbrush setup.

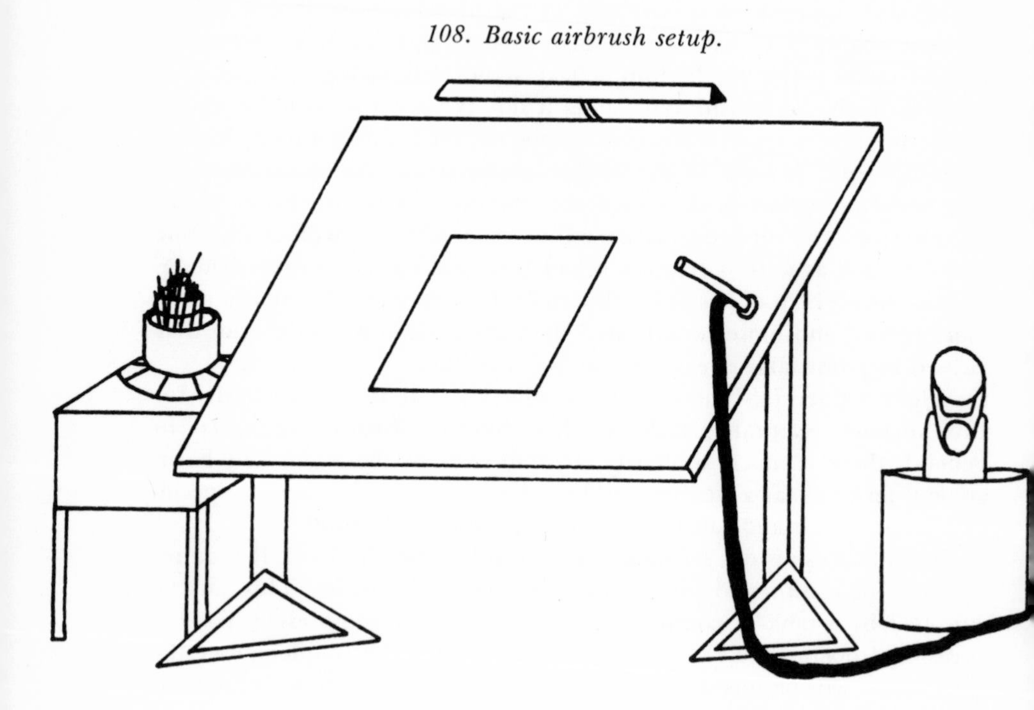

The main lever is the primary and most important control. Downward finger pressure will open the air valve and admit the air to the channel. A backward pull on the main lever acts to make the spray wider.

The air is carried through the channel to the tip assembly, which contains the spray regulator and where the color and air are mixed to form the spray. It is here that the color and air channels meet.

The color or paint is drawn from the color container, which can be a cup or glass jar and which is attached either to one side or below the main casing.

The needle is necessary to refine and control the spray and mixture. Its point blocks the opening in front of the part of the tip through which the color is released. The needle is moved backward by the action of the main lever. As the needle is moved back the opening in the tip becomes wider and more color is mixed into the air flow, resulting in a wider

109. Typical double action airbrush.

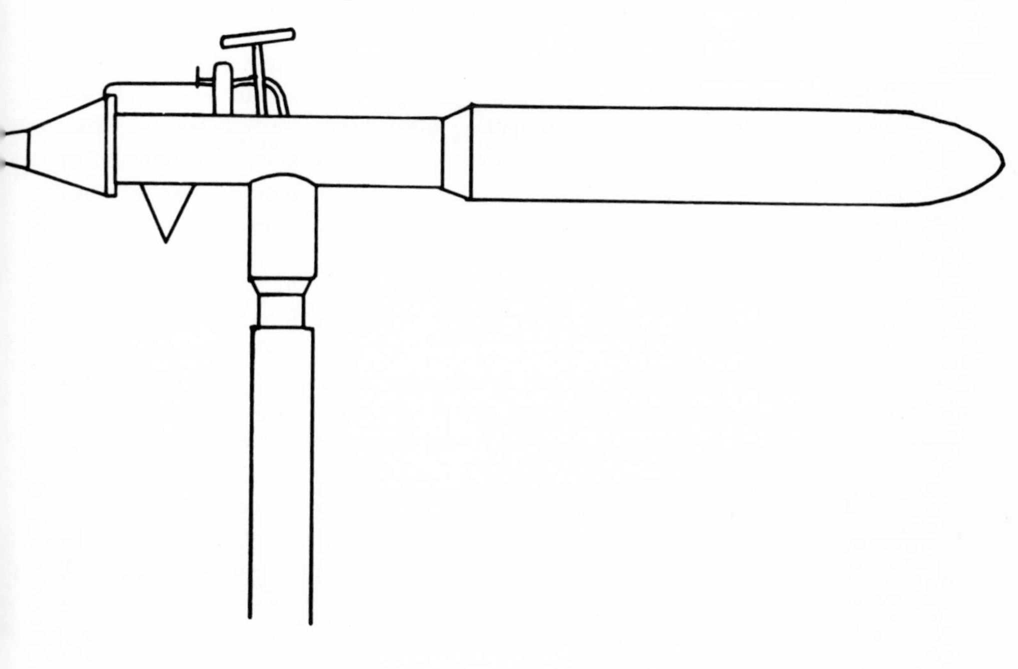

spray. To get a fine line, the needle must be as far forward as possible without completely blocking the opening of the tip. This actually is the second control offered by the main lever—the first being the opening and shutting of the flow of air.

CONTROLS

The artist has three controls in his use of the air brush. Two have already been mentioned. In one, downward pressure upon the main lever admits air to the air channel. There is back pressure applied to this main lever by a spring, which forces the valve closed when finger pressure is released, thus shutting off the flow of air. The second control is applied by the backward pull on the main lever, which forces back the needle and makes a wider spray. There is a spring here also, which pushes the needle forward when the backward finger pressure is released.

The third control is aim. It is a matter simply of pointing the air brush at the spot you want to retouch and getting the spray there. There is no sense to being able to make a fine line, a dot, or a wide tone and not being able to apply it where it is needed.

So the beginning air-brush artist must master these three controls. Practice—patient practice—is necessary. This is going to seem difficult when you first try it. The same feeling must have occurred to you when you started to roller skate, to ice skate, to ride a bicycle, or to engage in any other activity that required special physical dexerity. As practice enabled you to succeed in these endeavors, it will enable you also to succeed with airbrushing.

SETTING UP THE AIR BRUSH

If you intend to use the air brush, you must provide a permanent place for it. A temporary position, which you can set up and break down as you need it, is impractical. This is not the same as a box of oil paints and a folding easel.

First, there is the requirement for an air compressor or a large tank of compressed air. These are not easily portable and take up room. In addition, there must be a valve and hose connection, plus the length of hose to the air brush. These should be permanent. Taking them apart each time you want to use them will consume too much time and wear out the parts.

The easel or drawing table on which the work is to be done should be steady and substantial. A flimsy one will not give you the proper

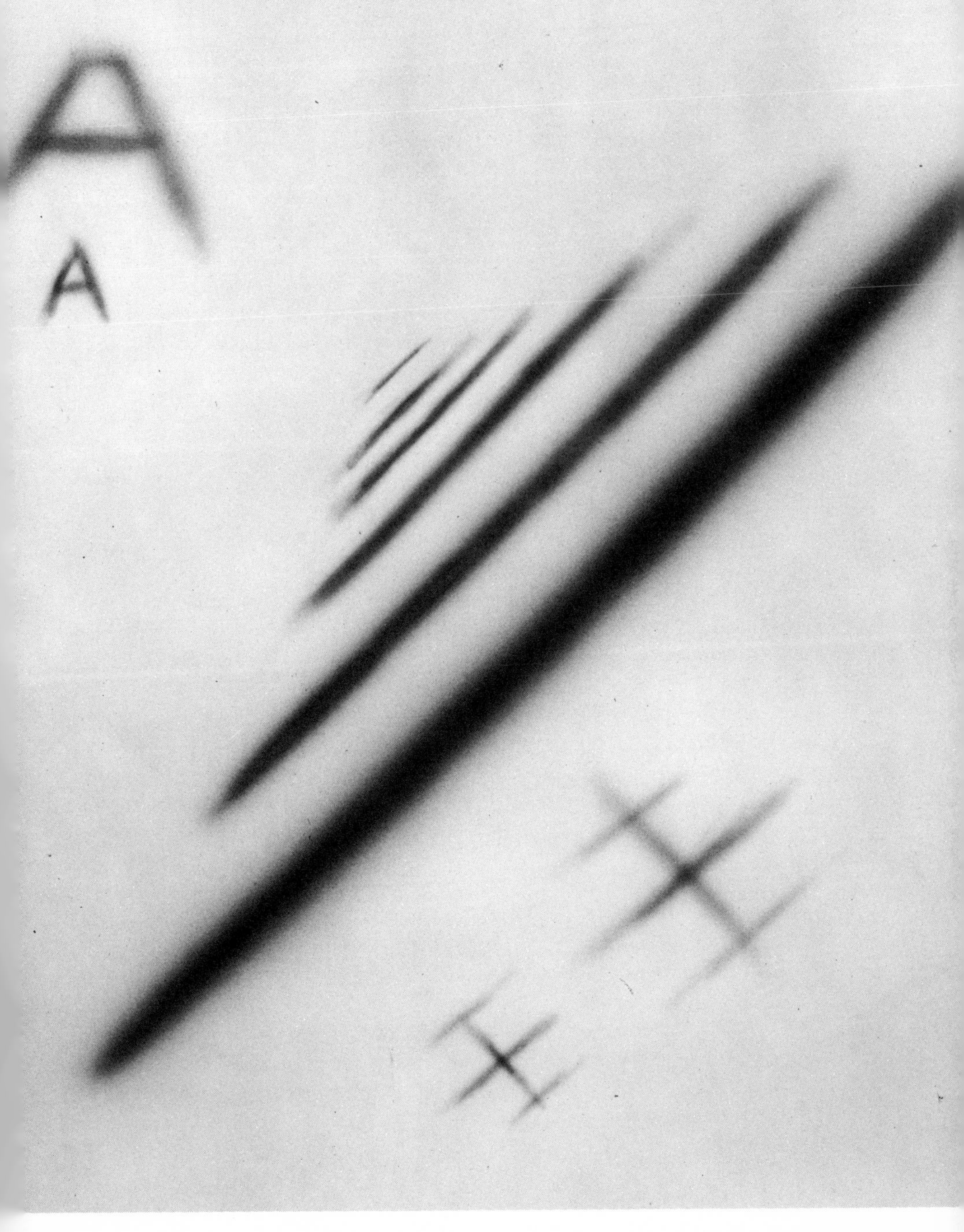

110. Lines of differing thicknesses made by the airbrush.

111. Varying shades of gray rendered by the airbrush in a cloudy effect.

support; you will be so concerned with whether or not it will hold up that you will be unable to concentrate properly upon your work. There should be some sort of an attachment here to hold the air brush when it is not in actual use.

Light is important. This may be supplied by a fluorescent attachment on the easel or by a north window light. Since the latter limits working to daylight hours, the artificial light source is a necessity.

In addition, you need some sort of cabinet to hold the multitude of colors, pastels, stencils, pencils, etc., that are also necessary.

Thus the amount of necessary furnishing requires the assignment of a permanent place for the operation of the air brush. This must be done before you can start to practice and learn to use the tool.

LEARNING TO USE THE AIR BRUSH

If you can get an experienced air-brush artist to take some time to introduce you to the use of the air brush, it will be of invaluable aid and set you on the right road. But, if this is not possible and you have to work by yourself, these instructions should help you.

You should start with a new air brush. You might think of picking up a secondhand one to start with, because it is cheaper and if you damage it, while learning, less is lost. This reasoning may be logical when applied to an automobile, but it does not follow with the air brush. The difference in price between a new and used air brush is not great. You are going to have enough trouble learning to use this instrument without having the additional difficulties of using an old one.

The secondhand or used air brush is usually one that has been discarded by its original owner, not because he wanted a new or better model, but because it no longer worked properly. An older, used air brush will give the operator more trouble than a new one. If the operator is experienced, he will know how to deal with these troubles. If he is a beginner, however, he will be presented with problems almost without solution. The parts of the air brush wear with use. This causes malfunctions. The needle, if bent at the point, will cause the spray to become coarse and grainy, to be off center, to be spotty, and to spit blobs of color on to the work. The opening of the tip is a very fine hole that must be perfectly round. This, too, can become worn. A minute piece of grit can adhere to the rim. It can be split by rough handling. This can cause spitting, grain, coarseness, and off-center sprays. Such minute flaws are difficult to find upon casual inspection. While it is possible for the

112. Airbrush effects obtained with the aid of a hand stencil.

experienced artist to correct these faults, the novice will be unable to cope with them.

So, the first rule is for you to obtain a new air brush. There is no reason, however, not to buy a secondhand compressor. If it is in working order, it will produce the same supply of compressed air as a new one. It may make more noise, use more electricity, and work harder, but it will not hinder your working and learning.

UNDERSTANDING HOW THE AIR BRUSH WORKS

Now in order to use this tool intelligently, you should be familiar with the way it works, with the functions of its various parts. What does the needle do? The tip? The main lever?

One way to understand the main principle behind the air brush is to consider the simple mouth sprayer. Here you have an instrument that consists of two hollow strawlike tubes at right angles to each other. The vertical tube is dipped into a jar of liquid. The horizontal tube is the mouthpiece, one end of which is placed between the lips, the other end of which is fixed adjacent to the upper end of the vertical tube, so that air blown through it passes over the opening. This passage of air causes a drop in atmospheric pressure at that point and draws the liquid out of the jar in the form of a spray. Physics students will recognize this as the Bernoulli effect.

A perfume atomizer, which uses a rubber bulb to force the air out of the tube, applies the same principle, as does the old-fashioned insecticide sprayer, which uses a pump to move the air. (These have been replaced today by the compressed gas spray cans, which operate under another principle and are not germane to this discussion.)

The air brush uses the same principle. Because a finer, more variable, and more accurate spray effect is required, more refinements are necessary. Here, as the air is forced through the air outlet and passes the color outlet, it draws the color from its reservoir and forms it into a spray.

This all takes place in the tip assembly. Here the air channel and the color channel come together. To direct and control the spray a fine needle is used. This needle passes through the color channel and emerges through the opening in the color tip. In its extreme forward position it blocks the opening. As it is drawn backward, this opening is widened so that a greater amount of color can pass through and a wider spray can be formed. The needle is drawn backward by the horizontal finger action of the main lever. This is the second control we spoke of earlier. Thus, to make a fine line, the needle should be at its extreme forward position, so that a minimal amount of color is released into the air stream. A wide spray, as we have noted before, results from an extreme back position of the needle. Intermediate results are obtained by using positions in between the extreme forward and extreme back positions.

FAMILIARITY

You should be familiar with the various parts of the air brush. One way to do this is to check the instructions that come with each air brush. Different ones, especially from different manufacturers, vary in construction and in the position and make-up of essential parts.

The operator should be able to take his air brush apart to clean, or fix, or replace worn parts. Air brushes can be returned to the factory for overhauling. This, however, takes time. There are air-brush mechanics, but they are few in number and can only be found in a few of the larger metropolitan areas. So, to overcome any slight difficulty that may arise in the operation of your air brush, you should be able to depend on your own efforts.

Actually, you should have little difficulty with a new air brush as long as it is kept clean.

MALFUNCTIONS

Trouble usually starts when the channels become clogged. Clogging very seldom occurs in the air channel; it is more common with the color channel. This is because some color dries in the passage during a period in which the air brush is not in use. Sometimes an undissolved grain of color material gets stuck there. When the air brush is working correctly, the color should be released in an even, smooth-flowing, uninterrupted spray. That is, as long as the main lever is depressed and the air valve is open. But when the spray is interrupted, when it stops without cause, and when it skips the probable cause is a blockage of the color channel.

Since the probable cause is a piece or grain of undissolved color, the obvious remedy is to flush water through the air brush, washing out the blockage. As soon as the spray becomes smooth and uninterrupted, you know you have gotten rid of the obstruction and the channel is clean. But sometimes you will find that, while you get a smooth spray with water, you get an unsteady one with color. This can mean the color mixture is too thick, that it is not properly mixed, or that it is too gritty and not adaptable for air-brush use. There are water colors that are made specifically for use with the air brush. These are the colors you should use. Your art dealer should have them.

113. Airbrush rendering with the effect of a third dimension and roundness have been obtained with the aid of stencils and shading. This shows the value of the airbrush in positive retouching.

Another place where an obstruction can occur is in the tip assembly, which usually consists of an outer tip, or spray regulator, and an inner one. The opening of the latter is pierced by the point of the needle. This rim of the tip must be perfectly round and the needle must come to a perfect point. If you get a fleck of grit or dry paint that adheres to either the rim of the tip or to the needle, it can cause uneven and intermittent spraying. It also can cause a deflection of the spray, spitting, and excessive grain.

The first attempt at correction should be to clean the tip and the needle with the passage of water, by spraying through the channels and tips until the obstructions are washed away. If this does not do the job, you must remove the needle from the air brush. Removing the needle is accomplished by unscrewing and removing the handle, which allows you access to the inside of the rear end of the air brush. Loosening a cap screw there will permit you to withdraw the needle. It should be examined to learn if any paint is sticking to its sides. If so, this can be removed by washing it with water. The point should be examined under magnification to see that it is not bent. If it is bent, and unless you are able to straighten it, a new one should be substituted. A bent needle can deflect the spray, cause spitting, grain, and spots.

The rim of the tip should also be examined under magnification. If the rim is not perfectly round, spray direction and control will be erratic. If encrusted dirt is there, it can be washed out. A swab of moist cotton, swirled around at the end of a toothpick can do the trick. If the tip is damaged, however, which can happen as a result of the insertion of a bent needle, through erosion, or wearing-out caused by gritty color, it should be replaced.

As the air brush is used, there will be wear and tear upon certain parts, which will have to be replaced. If it is used constantly, this will happen sooner than if it is only used occasionally. But, with normal care, attention to cleaning, and the use of clean, nongritty colors, there should be little or no trouble with a new air brush.

GAINING FAMILIARITY WITH THE AIR BRUSH

Familiarity is an important word. You must become familiar with this instrument. We have discussed how it works and the troubles you will have before obtaining a proper understanding of the tool. Perhaps we repeated ourselves to emphasize some points. But, the really important familiarization is that of your hand to the air brush. The hand has to become so familiar with it that the air brush becomes an extension of the fingers. This requires much practice.

You can start by putting a clean sheet of paper on the easel, adding some black water color to the air-brush cup, and getting to know how the air brush feels by spraying in shades and washes, making broad lines and fine lines, and by target practice. Target practice is done by drawing a number of circles on the paper, preferably by air brush, then trying to shoot a dot of color into the center of the circle. This is to develop your aim, which, as we mentioned before, is the third control over the air brush.

When you first try to use the air brush, you will probably find that you have a tendency to overcontrol. This will cause the air brush to run away with you. As you keep on practicing, you will learn how to depress the main lever to get the right amount of air and how to release it when you want to shut off the flow of air. The secret here is smoothness of action. The pressure of the finger must be gentle and firm. You will learn how to use the same finger, at the same time, to pull the main lever back far enough to get the width of spray you desire and not to pull it back so far that you get too much paint on your work. You will learn how to release this back pressure delicately to allow the main lever to move forward under your control so that you can cause the spray to become finer. Never allow the main lever to snap back to its forward position. This can cause the needle to split the tip.

Experiment, try to draw pictures, create designs, and make small paintings. Try to write with the air brush and try lettering. Do all this freehand. It matters little how well you draw, or letter, or paint. The important thing is to gain control over the air brush.

Hand stencils are a valuable aid, and are, in fact, necessary. You should not try to use them until after you gain some degree of control. Stencils will shield those areas you do not want to be affected by the spray. They will allow you to cut around figures and to make sharp lines and outlines. They can be cut out to any desired shape from stiff, flexible cardboard. Old cut films can be used, as can stiff celluloid. The material used must be pliable enough to bend under the gentle pressure required to hold it against the work, while not so thin that it will vibrate under the force of the air spray.

To learn how to use them and to get used to them, you can practice making squares, rectangles, and cubes, as well as circles and cones, using the stencil to make the outline, then shading for depth and three-dimensional effect.

When you feel that you have mastered the air brush to a reasonable degree, when you can make it do what you want it to, you can start working on practice photo prints. As you look over the practice print, assign yourself air-brush problems. Cover a background. Make a new one. Tone down highlights. Burn in the corners. Vignette with white opague. Whatever air brush improvement or correction the print might call for, try to do it. If you do not succeed, try again and again and again until you get there.

Should you find yourself short of practice prints, you can always remove the old work with water, swabbing it off with wet cotton, then rewashing the print.

To summarize and repeat, the only way to become proficient in the use of the air brush is to practice. It demands the investment of time, dedication, work, and patience.

CHAPTER 9

CONCLUSION

The basic steps necessary to create, or rather re-create a new, restored print from a damaged photograph, old or new, follow a definite order. First, there is the pre-copy step of cleaning and preparing the original for copying. There is the second step, that of making the copy negative. The copy negative can be improved by retouching, which is the third step. The fourth step is that of making the workprint. This is retouched, airbrushed, and restored. Then it is recopied and final prints are made. Further artwork and retouching can be done to them.

In each one of these steps, work can be done to contribute to the restoration and finishing of the job. Work or corrections that can be accomplished in the primary steps will save work in the later stages. A few minutes spent in cleaning an original can save hours in retouching; a little work on the copy negative can save many times that work on the workprint.

The photo-restorer is a composite of photographer, retoucher, and artist. He wears three hats. It is possible for him to be more skilled in one of these than in the other two. If that is true, he will lean more heavily on that skill to finish his work.

Photo-restoration is a skill that can only be acquired by doing, working, practicing, studying, and experience. It requires diligence. You have to gain skill by working by yourself. There are, to my knowledge, no schools or courses available. The old-timers in this craft learned their trade via the route of apprenticeship. This is not practical today. However, if you can make the acquaintance of an experienced photo-restorer

Typical types of restoration jobs, before and after.

114. (ABOVE) Image on an old tintype.

115. (BELOW) Copy restoration, in the form of a vignetted bust portrait.

116. (ABOVE) *Torn crayon-type enlargement.*

117. (BELOW) *Copy restoration, showing a complete rebuilding of the damaged areas and cropping to eliminate the effect of too much body area in the print.*

118. (ABOVE) *A photograph that has been damaged by paint streaks and ink.*

119. (BELOW) *A cropped restoration print.*

120. Images on an old postcard type print.

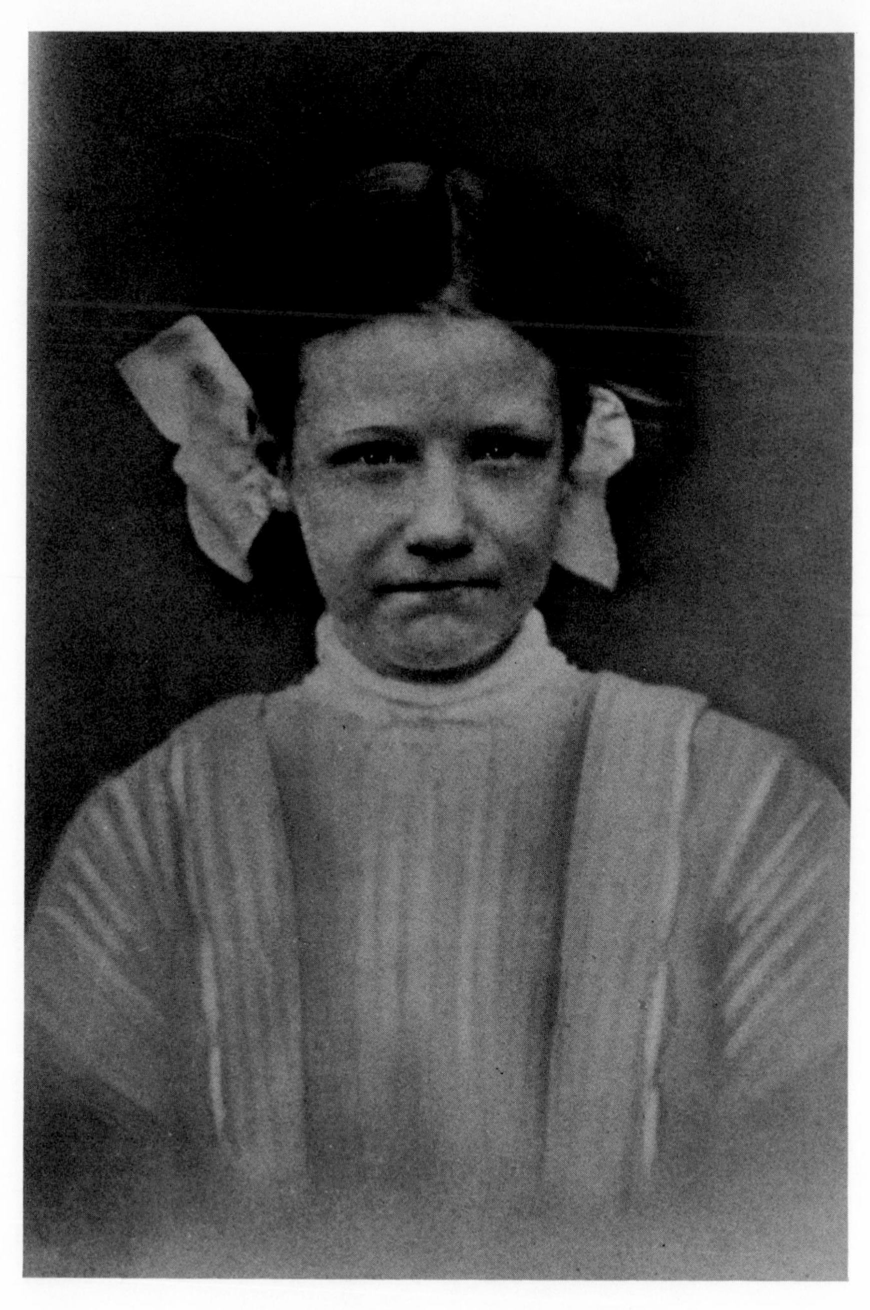

121. Copy restoration of the girl, as a bust portrait.

or a portrait photographer who has much experience with this work, he could give you advice and counseling that can be of great help to you.

Photo-restoration exists only as a professional service that satisfies a consumer's desire. As such, it can be considered a specialized branch of professional photography.

There are many sentimental and emotional reasons why people want damaged photos repaired, rejuvenated, or restored. This type of work is particular, demanding, and time-consuming. The successful photo-restorer must have a liking for it or it becomes boring, and the workmanship suffers.

But when you take an old, torn, battered, and weary photograph and create a beautiful new one from it, there is a feeling of pride and accomplishment that is equal to that of creating a beautiful painting from a clean canvas or making a fine, award-winning photograph.

Today, there is only a handful of photo-restorers practicing their craft. They reach the public, or rather, the public reaches them through photo studios, camera shops, photo-finishers, picture framers, or art galleries, who act as their agents or middlemen. Some employ canvassers or door-to-door agents, but they are disappearing.

There is room in the profession for many more photo-restorers. Damaged personal photographs—the raw material—number in the millions. Those that people treasure enough to have restored and to pay for restoring make up a good percentage of that number. This is a situation where, if the service were more readily available, there would be more demand for it.

If you can do the job, you will get the work. And, if you work at it, you will learn to do the job.

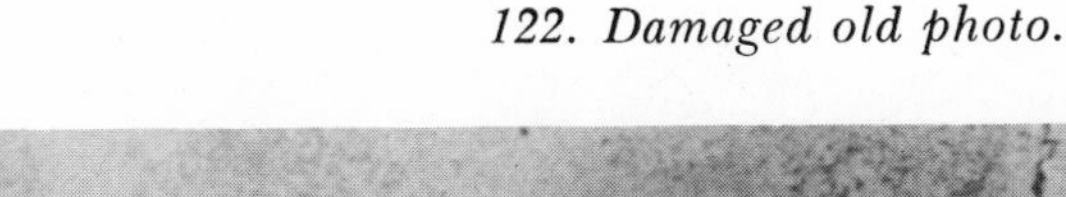

122. Damaged old photo.

123. Copy restoration with shoulders and bust finished with a full background.

124. (ABOVE) *The image on a very small original, which shows a lot of grain when enlarged.*

125. (BELOW) *The copy restoration, with the grain killed by airbrush work and details in the dress brought out by airbrush and eraser lines.*

126. (ABOVE) *Another original with a small image.*

127. (BELOW) *The finished restoration, with the suit built out to the edges of the print, facial details and outlines brought out by airbrush work and retouching.*

INDEX

INDEX

Abrasions, *see* Scratches
Age lines, *see* Facial corrections
Air brush, air brushing, 14, 16, 18-20, 22, 25, 35, 39, 49, 53, 55, 66, 67, 77, 79, 80, 85-90, 92, 94, 100, 107, 111-14, 115, 119-20, 124-25, 130-31, 134, 139, 140, 154, 161, 163-76
 blocking with, 86-87
 construction of, 164-66, 171-72
 controls on, 166
 malfunctions, 172-74
 setup, 166-69
 using, 169-71, 174-76
Alcohol, 51
Ambrotype, 45, 47-49, 72
Ammonia, 26, 32, 55, 56
Aniline dyes, *see* Paint
Artgum, 26, 27, 32, 108, 125
Artistic ability, 22-23, 77, 107, 133
Art tools, *see* Retouching
"As-is" restoration, 123, 125

Background, 22, 78, 80, 82, 83-87, 102, 114, 123-25
 correcting, 83-87, 123-25
 removing, 124
Backings (*also see* Mounts), 39, 53
Bellows, 58
Black spots, 83-85, 109, 110, 119, 139, 141
Blacks, increasing, 79
Bleach, bleaching, 29, 30, 80, 102
Blemishes, 22, 24, 39, 115, 145
Blending, 80
Blocking out, 80, 85-87
Borders, 63
Breaks, 13, 14, 26, 27, 34-35, 51, 56, 77, 122
Building-in, 119
Burning-in, 97, 160

Camera, *see* Copy camera
Carbon tetrachloride, 30
Cases, 46, 48, 49, 69-70
Chamois cloth, 109
Chemical deterioration, 13, 25-33, 47
Cleaning, 14, 24-33, 46, 49, 52, 55, 56, 91, 125
Clothing, 87-89, 101-102, 114-15, 125-34
 clothing prints, 133
 correcting on negative, 87-89
 correcting on workprint, 125-34
Color, 20, 46, 55, 80, 92, 154

Color print, 46, 55-57
Commercial film, *see* Films
Contrast, 51, 68, 69, 72, 100-103, 140, 154
Copy, copying, *Passim,* 58-76
ambrotypes, 72
daguerreotypes, 69-72
faded prints, 73
grained prints, 73-75
large prints, 74, 75-76
tintypes, 72-73
Copyboard, 18, 59, 61, 62-63, 69, 72, 73
Copy camera, 18, 35, 42, 58-59, 61, 63-66, 72, 73
enlarging with, 64-66
focusing with, 63-64
reducing with, 64
Copy print, *see* Workprint
Cracks, 13, 14, 16, 26, 29, 34-35, 37, 44, 51, 53-54, 56, 77, 83, 89, 110, 115, 121-22, 134, 138-39
Crayon enlargements, 45, 53-55
Cropping, 17, 22, 58, 63, 93, 160
Curled photos, 35-36, 51, 62, 75
Cyanide, as bleaching agent, 80

Daguerrotype, 13, 45, 46-47, 69-72
copying, 69-72
pre-copy treatment, 46-47
Damage, *see* Deterioration
Dampness, *see* Moisture
Darkroom, 18
Density, increasing, reducing, 79, 80, 83
Detail, 14, 69, 101, 102, 123, 140, 144
rebuilding, 140
Deterioration, 13, 25-39, 51, 136-40
chemical, 13, 25-33, 51
physical, 13, 34-39, 51
Developer, 72, 100
Developing, 18, 100
Diffusion, 17, 98, 103, 160
Discoloration, 13, 67
Distortion, 51, 59
Dirt, 25-29, 33, 47, 49, 52, 77, 99, 102
Dodging, 17, 22, 97-98, 100, 160
Drawing board, 20, 166

Elimination of background, 80, 124
Emulsion, protecting, 18, 26, 27, 29, 30, 36, 38, 44-45, 49, 51, 56
Enlargers, 18, 67
Enlarging in copying, 64-66, 79, 95, 103-104
"step-up" method, 104
Eraser, erasing, 26-27, 29, 32-33, 108, 125, 140, 144
Etching, 25, 77, 79-80, 83, 109, 119, 135, 139
Exudation, 13, 14, 32-33
Eyeglasses, 135
Eyes, *see* Facial corrections

Facial corrections, 89-90, 102-103, 114, 115-17, 134-36, 136-50
on negative, 89-90
on workprint, 115-17, 134-150
specific features, 136-50
Faded, fading, 13, 29, 53, 67, 68, 73, 100, 140
Ferrotyping, 92
Filmholders, 18
Films, 13-14, 22, 58, 66-68, 100, 154
cut vs. roll, 66
for copying, 58, 66-67, 72, 73, 75, 76
for recopying, 154
size, 58, 67
Filters, 13-14, 18, 22, 67-68, 72, 73, 75, 76
Final print, *see* Print
Finishes, 41, 44, 55-56, 92
Fire, 13, 30
Flattening, 51, 52, 53
Focusing camera, *see* Copy camera
Food stains (*also see* Stains), 30
Framing, 162
Friction tape, 51-53
Frisket, cutout, 86, 124
F/stops, for copying, 64

Goldtone, 161
Glaze, 41-42
Grain, 39-45, 104, 161
Grained prints, 73-75
Grained surface, *see* Surface, Finishes
Grease, 25
Ground glass back, 63, 72, 73, 74, 76
Guidelines, 62-63

Hair, *see* Facial corrections
"Halo effect," 97, 124
Hand-colored prints, 46, 55-56
Hand stencil, 86

Highlights, 111, 116, 135, 140
Holes, 26, 28, 34, 39, 49

Image, brightening, 49-51, 70-72
India ink (*also see* Stains), 119
Ink marks, 13, 30

Kneaded eraser, *see* Artgum
Knife, *see* Etching

Lacquer, 41-42
Lens, use of, 64
Lights, lighting, 32, 35, 41, 50-51, 59, 61, 70-72, 73, 74, 76, 136, 138, 169
"Likeness," 102-103, 117, 135, 146
Lines, 51, 90, 115, 140
Lint, 51
Lips, *see* Facial corrections
Lipstick marks (*also see* Stains), 30
"Local control," 139

Mask, masking, 17, 24, 63, 86, 95, 124
  cutout mask (frisket) , 86
  vignette mask, 96
Mat, 47
Missing parts, prints, 122
Moisture, 13, 30
Mounted prints, 45, 51-52, 161
Mounts, mounting, 30, 35-36, 45, 51-53, 56, 161
  for copying, 62, 69, 72
Mouth, *see* Facial corrections

"Natural" faults, 136, 140-46
Negative, copy, 14, 16, 22, 24-25, 41, 58, 66, 67, 68-69, 72, 73, 77-90, 91, 94, 99, 100, 107, 122, 133, 136, 140, 177
  judging 68-69, 82-90
  size, 58, 67, 79, 107
  retouching, 77-90
Negative, recopy (restored), 18, 104, 133
Nose, *see* Facial corrections

Oil paints, *see* Paints, Cleaning
Opaquing, 25, 80, 85-87, 88, 92, 115, 119, 122, 124, 140, 144
  "stop-and-go" method, 140
Orthochromatic film, *see* Films
Oxidation, 13, 32

Paint, 22, 30, 48, 49, 55, 78, 80, 85, 107, 110, 114, 119, 122, 124-25, 140, 154, 161, 172, 175
  air brush colors, 172, 175
  spotting colors, 110
Panchromatic film, *see* Films
Papers, types of, 18, 49, 92, 100-103, 154
Pastel enlargements, 46, 53-55
Pastels, 109-110, 122, 130, 169
Paste-up, 133-34
Petroleum jelly, 33, 42, 45, 50, 56
Photographic tools, *see* Retouching
Pitting, 47, 49
Polarized screens, 74-75
Pre-copy work, 14-16, 24-57, 69, 91, 177
  cleaning, *see* Cleaning
  on ambrotype, 47-49
  on daguerreotype, 46-47
  on color prints, 56-57
  on crayon (pastel) enlargements, 53-55
  on hand-colored prints, 55-56
  on mounted originals, 51-52
  on tintypes, 49-51
  on unmounted originals, 52-53
Print, *Passim, also see* Workprint, Recopy print
Print, color, 46
Print, copy, *see* Workprint
Print, final (*also see* Recopy print), 14, 16, 18, 24, 91, 103, 104-105, 153-62
Print, reproduction (*also see* Workprint), 16, 92, 98
Printing frame, 35, 36, 38, 53, 73
Processing, 18, 22, 29

Recopy, recopying, 14, 18, 23, 91, 153-62, 177
  method, 154
  printing, 154-60
  reasons for, 153-54
  size, 154
Recopy print (*also see* Print), 104, 105, 153-62
Redeveloping, 29
Reducing in copying, 64
Reflectors, 61, 73-74
Repainting, 49
Reproduction print, *see* Print, Workprint

Restored negative, *see* Negative
Retouching, *Passim*
  analysis of, 118-19
  on copy negative, 77-90
  on final print, 161
  on workprint, 77, 79, 91, 99, 105-152
  plan for, 114-15
  purposes of, 22, 35, 106-107
  the face, 134-50
  tools for, 17-18, 77-79, 80-82, 107-114
Retouching pencil, 78, 107-108, 119, 121, 138, 140
  carbon, 107
  lead, 108
Retouching stand, 80-82

Scars, *see* Facial corrections
Scratches, 13, 27
Secondary workprint, 133
Sepia print, 161
Shade, shading, 111
Shadows, 41-42, 109, 111, 140, 141
Sharpness, 68, 98-99, 135
Shellac, 42-44, 45, 51, 55, 56
Skin, *see* Facial corrections
Soap, 26, 30, 55, 56
Softening, 80, 141
Spots, 16, 22, 51, 67, 82, 83, 89, 109, 115, 134, 139
Spotting, 22, 66, 79-80 108, 110-111, 161
Spotting brush, 14, 20, 22, 63, 77, 78, 83, 88-89, 110, 119, 121, 122, 125, 139
"Sprayover," 125
Stains, 13, 29-30, 47, 49, 55, 67-68, 72, 77, 99, 102, 120, 134, 139-40
Stencil, 86, 124-25, 131, 175
Storage, 13
Strength of print, 99-100
Surface (*also see* Emulsion Finishes), 18, 41, 49, 55-56, 92, 160
Swabbing, 27

Tears, 14, 37, 44, 56, 77, 110, 122
  retouching, 122
Tempera, *see* Paint
Texture, *see* Surface, Finishes
Texture screens, 161
Tint, 111, 161
Tintype, 49-51, 72-73
Tone, 18, 20, 29, 99, 111, 161
Tones, 49, 92, 99, 111, 124
Tools, *see* Retouching
Tortillon stump, 39, 107, 109, 111, 120, 130, 140, 161
Trim, trimming (*also see* cropping), 53
Turpentine, 30, 55

Unmounted prints, 52-53

Varnish, 55
View camera, *see* Copy camera
View screen, *see* Ground glass back
Vignetting, 17, 22, 86, 94-96, 115, 124, 160
  "dark vignetting," 97
  on workprint, 94-96, 115
  mask for, 96

Washing, *see* Cleaning
Water color, *see* Paint, Cleaning
White cards (in place of lights), 74
White spots, 83-85, 107, 110, 119, 140
Workprint (Copy print, Reproduction print), 14, 16, 17-18, 39, 67, 69, 77, 80, 82, 85, 91-105, 106-152, 153, 154, 177
  as final print, 91, 92
  burning-in, 97
  contrast in, 100-103
  corrections on, 123-36
  cropping, 93
  detail in, 105
  dodging, 97-98, 100
  facial corrections on, 134-36, 136-50
  for recopying, 92
  judging, 98-103, 150-52
  retouching, 106-152
  secondary, 133
  sharpness of, 98-99
  size of, 103-105, 107, 150
  techniques of producing, 93-98
  tools for, 107-114
  vignetting, 94-96, 118-19
Wrinkles, 22, 90, 141